Encountering Christ in the Sacraments

A Primary Source Reader

Robert Feduccia Jr.

saint mary's press

The publishing team included Gloria Shahin, editorial director; Joanna Dailey, development editor. Prepress and manufacturing coordinated by the production departments of Saint Mary's Press.

Cover Image @ The Crosiers / Gene Plaisted, OSC

Printed in the United States of America

1362

ISBN 978-1-59982-046-0, print

Contents

Excerpt from "Homily of Jean Vanier at Lambeth Vigil (Second Service)," by Jean Vanier

Introduction

Dip. Scratch, scratch, scratch. Dip. Scratch, scratch. Stop.

Brother Declan laid down his quill pen and squinted at the bright sunlight streaming through the windows of the scriptorium ("writing room") of his medieval monastery. He straightened his back and massaged his wrists and fingers. Copying manuscripts was arduous, time-consuming, and tedious work. The pen, basically a goose feather with a sharpened point, could hold only a drop of ink—enough to make a few letters on the parchment, but no more. It required constant replenishment from the ink bottle—much as we, thought Declan, require constant replenishment from the fountains of salvation, the Sacraments. (He happened to be copying a manuscript from the great scholar and sacramental theologian Peter Lombard.)

Declan closed his eyes for a moment and recalled what his old abbot often said: "Brothers, you do not do this work for our monastery alone. Your manuscripts may be sent with missionaries to far-off places to help evangelize new Christians. Through your work, you are preserving the Sacred Tradition of the Church for future generations."

I hope, Declan thought as he once again picked up his pen, that future generations appreciate what we are doing. Dip. Scratch, scratch, scratch. Dip. Scratch, scratch. Dip. . . .

As readers of this book of primary source excerpts on the Sacraments, we are only one of the "future generations" for which the original authors, and copyists, labored. As Jesus himself said in the Gospel of John, "Others have done the work, and you are sharing the fruits of their work" (John 4:38). Thanks to those who have treasured these texts before us, we hold in our hands a small selection of a vast library, scattered throughout the world (and on the Internet, as well), of Church teaching and reflection on the Sacraments.

The liturgy and the Sacraments are at the core of the Church's existence. They have shaped the Church's life since the time of the Apostles and have been continually pondered and discovered anew by succeeding generations. Some of the excerpts you will read in this text are old. These include the excerpts from Saint John Damascene, Saint Cyprian of Carthage, Peter Lombard, Saint John Chrysostom, and Saint Catherine of Siena. Many are Church documents from the twentieth century, particularly from the Second Vatican Council (1962–1965), which describe the renewal of sacramental rites within the context of the renewal of Christian life. Excerpts from contemporary theologians echo and expand on these themes.

The Sacraments are life-giving, because in them we encounter the Risen Christ. To be truly understood, they must be lived. With this in mind, a contemporary story about a personal encounter with Christ, either autobiographical or illustrated in fiction, has been included for each Sacrament. Perhaps these stories of personal encounter will inspire you to live the Sacraments more deeply in your own life.

When Augustine (354–430) (before he was a saint) was deep in thought one day, he heard a child chanting, "Take up and read. Take up and read." He opened the Scriptures and began his journey to encounter Christ. What more need be said? Take up and read!

Part 1
The Sacramental Nature of the Church

1 Sacrament: Visible Sign, Invisible Grace

Introduction

The Seven Sacraments are gifts to us from Jesus. In the Seven Sacraments, Jesus gave the Church seven unique ways to encounter him. Baptism, Anointing of the Sick, and, of course, the Eucharist are examples of such encounters. Over the years, the Church, in study and prayer, has reflected on these and the other Sacraments. The result of this reflection is an area of theology called sacramental theology. This chapter has a reading that has been uniquely influential in the area of sacramental theology. When Peter Lombard (c. 1100–1160) wrote the fourth book of *The Sentences* in the twelfth century, he gave the Church an understanding of the meaning of **sacrament** that would influence the Church's official teaching on the Sacraments, later defined at the Council of Trent in the sixteenth century (1545–1563), and so would provide a language for sacramental theology that endures today.

In this reading you will see that Lombard defines what a sacrament is. In the famous *Baltimore Catechism,* most commonly used in the United States in the early and mid-twentieth century, *Sacrament* was defined as "an outward sign, instituted by Christ to give grace." As you read Lombard's definition, you will notice that his definition of *Sacrament* was a model. In addition to his

Sacrament An efficacious and visible sign of God's grace, instituted by Christ and entrusted to the Church, by which divine life is dispensed to us. The Seven Sacraments are Baptism, the Eucharist, Confirmation, Penance and Reconciliation, Anointing of the Sick, Matrimony, and Holy Orders.

definition of a Sacrament, he also inspired sacramental theology by providing the Church with a clarification of the meaning of the Sacraments and an understanding about the words and things used in sacramental celebrations.

Lombard explains that there are three reasons Christ gave the Sacraments to the Church: (1) humiliation, (2) erudition, and (3) exercitation (ex-ser-see-TAY-shun). Humans are humbled because the Sacraments are made of simple things that could be considered beneath our dignity to use. Bread, wine, water, and oil are all simple things, but God has chosen to use them for our salvation. It requires humility on our part to give ourselves over to them. The second reason, erudition, has to do with matters of great learning. As we meditate and reflect on the Sacraments, God teaches us about himself. Finally, Lombard explains, the Sacraments were instituted for exercitation. This word roughly means "exercise." The Sacraments are activities that engage both the body and the soul. Because they are actions, they hold our attention and keep us from distractions.

Another important distinction with lasting effect upon sacramental theology is Lombard's description of the Sacraments as involving words and things. Today's sacramental theology uses the term *matter* for "things." These things, or matter, are the materials used in the Sacraments. For example, water is used as the material, the matter, in Baptism. The words, or the form, used in Baptism is, "I baptize you in the name of the Father, and of the Son, and of the Holy Spirit." When the proper things and the correct words are used by the appropriate minister with the intention to do what the Church does in celebrating a Sacrament, the Sacrament is said to be valid. This is the official teaching of the Church, and Lombard held a place of particular influence in crafting that teaching as he reflected on the Sacraments.

Because of its medieval language and structure, this is a challenging reading; but without the sacramental theology of Peter Lombard, any study of primary sources on the topic of the Sacraments would be severely lacking.

Excerpt from *The Sentences: Book 4*

By Peter Lombard

Chapter I

On the Sacraments.

For the Samaritan, appropriating the wounded (man), for his curing employed the bindings of the Sacraments, (cf. Luke 10:10) because against the wounds of original and actual sin God has instituted the remedies of the Sacraments. Concerning which there first occurs four (questions) to be considered: what is a Sacrament; why (was it) instituted; in what (things) does it consist and is confected; and what is the distance between the Sacraments of the Old and New Law.

Chapter II

What is a Sacrament.

"A Sacrament is a sign of a sacred thing."[1] However a sacrament is also said (to be) a *sacred secret*, just as there is said (to be) a sacrament of the Divinity, so that a sacrament is a *sacred thing signifying* and the *sacred thing signified* [*sacrum signans et sacrum signatum*]; but now one

> ❝ *A Sacrament is the visible form of an invisible grace.* ❞

deals with the sacrament, according to which it is a *sign* [signum]. — Likewise,[2] "A Sacrament is the visible form of an invisible grace."

Chapter III

What is a sign.

"A sign, however, is the thing beside the **species**, which it bears upon the senses, causing something else out of itself to come into (one's) thinking."[3]

Chapter IV

How sign and Sacrament differ.

"Of signs, however, some are *natural,* as smoke signifying fire; others *given*";[4] and of those which are *given,* certain ones are Sacraments, certain ones not. For every Sacrament is a sign, but not conversely. A Sacrament bears the **similitude** of that thing, of which it is a sign. For if the Sacraments did not have the similitude of the things, of which they are Sacraments, they would not *properly* be said (to be) Sacraments." For Sacrament is properly said (to be) that which is so great a sign of the grace of God and the form of invisible grace, that it bears its image and exists as (its) cause. Therefore not only for the grace of signifying have the Sacraments been instituted, but also (for that) of sanctifying. For those things which have only been instituted for the grace of signifying, are solely signs, and not Sacraments; just as were the carnal sacrifices and ceremonial observances of the Old Law, which never could make the ones offering just; because, as the Apostle says, (Heb. 9:13) *the blood of goats and bulls and the sprinkling of the ashes of a heifer use to sanctify the polluted* [iniquitos] *as regards the cleansing forth of the flesh,* not of the soul. For that pollution was contact with the dead. Whence (St.) Augustine (says):[5] "Nothing other do I understand the *pollution,* which the Law cleanses, but contact with a dead man, whom he who had touched *was unclean for seven days;* but he was purified according to the Law on the third and seventh day, and he was clean", to now enter the Temple. Those (sacraments) of the Law sometimes used to cleanse even leprosy from the corporal (man); but never has anyone out of *the works of the Law* been justified, as the Apostle says, (Rom. 3:20; Gal. 2:16) even if they were done in faith and charity. Why? because God imposed them as a liability [in servitutem], not for justification, and so that they would be a

> **Sign and Sacrament**
>
> A "sign," for Lombard, is an indicator that something else is at work. He says that smoke is an indicator of fire. A Sacrament, on the other hand, does more. A Sacrament is an indicator of God's presence, and it also *brings* God's presence.

> **species** When speaking of Sacraments, the term *species* refers to the material used in the Sacraments. It is another word for "matter" or "things."
>
> **similitude** A similarity or likeness to something else.

figure of the future, (Rom. 5:14) willing, that these be offered to Himself rather than to idols. Therefore they were *signs,* but nevertheless [tamen] in the Scriptures they are also often called *Sacraments,* because they were signs of a sacred thing, which they certainly did not insure [utique non praestabant]. Moreover those the Apostle says (Acts 15:10) (are) the *works of the Law,* which have been instituted only for the grace of signifying, and/or as a burden.

Chapter V

Why the Sacraments have been instituted.

Moreover out of a threefold cause have the Sacraments been instituted: on account of *humiliation, erudition, exercitation.* On account of *humiliation* indeed, so that while a man in the sensible things, which by nature are below him, subjects himself in reverence [se reverendo] out of the Creator's precept, out of this humility and obedience he pleases God more and merits before [apud] Him, by whose command [imperio] he seeks salvation in (the things) inferior to himself, even if not *from them,* but (rather) *through them* from God.—On account of *erudition* have they also been instituted, so that through that which is discerned [cernitur] outwardly in the visible species, the mind may be instructed to acknowledge the invisible virtue, which is within. For the Man, who before sin used to see God without a medium, was dulled through sin to such an extent, that he was unable to grasp divine (things), except by human exercitations [exercitatus].—On account of *exercitation* have they similarly been instituted: because, since man cannot be free from public duties [otiosus], there is proposed to him a useful and **salubrious exercitation** in the Sacraments, by which he may turn aside from [declinet] vain and noxious occupation. For not easily is he grasped by a tempter, who has time for good exercise [bono vacat exercitio]; whence (St.) Jerome[6] warns: "Always do some work, so that the devil will find you occupied." "Moreover there are three species of *exercitations:* one pertains to the *edification of the soul;* the other

> **salubrious exercitation**
>
> This is a medieval way of saying "health-giving exercise." Lombard is writing about the health that Sacraments give to both the soul and the body.

to the *foment of the body*, another to the *subversion of both.*"—Therefore though apart from the Sacraments, to which God has not

> **foment** To stir up. Lombard uses the word to mean that the Sacraments "stir up" or occupy the body because they are visible.

bound His own power, He can grant grace to a man, He has instituted the Sacraments from the aforesaid causes. "Moreover there are two (parts), in which a Sacrament consists, that is *words* and *things: words*, as the invocation of the Trinity; *things,* as water, oil and (things) of this kind."

Endnotes

Chapters I–IV:

1. (St.) Augustine, *On the City of God*, Bk. X, ch. 5, and *Against the Adversaries of the Law and Prophets*, ch. 9, n. 34.—A little more below this after *just as* [sicut] the Vatican text and very many editions omit *there is said (to be)* [dicitur], disagreeing with the codices.
2. (St.) Augustine, *Questions on the Pentateuch*, Bk. III, q. 84.
3. (St.) Augustine, *On Christian Doctrine*, Bk. II, ch. 1, n. 1; in which text codex C and the editions, except 6, have *cognition* [cognitionem] in place of *thinking* [cogitationem], in disagreement even with the original.
4. *Loc. cit.*, n. 2. The following passage is from (St.) Augustine, *Epistle 98* (alias 23), "To Boniface the Bishop," n. 9.
5. *Questions on the Pentateuch*, Bk. IV, q. 33, n. 10, according to the sense, where it refers to Num. 19:11.—In this quote before *clean* [mundus] codices C and D and very many editions add *thus* [ita].

Chapter V:

6. *Epistle 125* (alias 4), "To Rusticus," n. 11.—Those which proceed in this chapter and the two following passages have been taken from Hugo (of St. Victor), *Summa of Sentences*, tr. 4, ch. 1, and *On Sacraments*, Bk. I, p. IX, ch. 3.

For Reflection

1. Peter Lombard says Sacraments bring "invisible" grace. Why would it be important for humans to have something visible that brings the invisible presence of God? Please explain.

2. After reading this chapter, how would you define a Sacrament?

3. Lombard offers three reasons the Sacraments were given to the Church. Explain the meaning each of these reasons has for you.

2 The Sacraments: Union with Christ

Introduction

"Christ is the Light of nations": this quotation begins *Dogmatic Constitution on the Church (Lumen Gentium, 1964)*. When the Church issues a dogmatic statement such as this, the statement represents an unchanging statement of truth. This document from the Second Vatican Council is the Church's authoritative teaching about the Church's self-identity. It begins with a statement about Christ because he is the reason for the Church. Jesus lived and taught among the Apostles, and he left them with ways to continue his presence throughout the ages. If Christ is the light of the nations, then the Church, the People of God, is the light as well, because Christ has entrusted us with his mission of proclaiming the Kingdom of God and reconciling all people to God.

This document on the Church makes clear its two purposes. First, it intends to reflect upon the nature of the Church and uses images of stability, unity, and dynamism to describe this nature. It affirms that there has been an unbroken line from Jesus, to the Apostles, to the Pope and bishops, to the Church of today. This unbroken line indicates the Church's stability and endurance despite times of great difficulty. In highlighting the Church's unity, this document describes the Church as the Body of Christ and also as the Bride of Christ. There is only one, single Body of Christ or Bride of Christ. Therefore, there is an essential unity among the members of the Church. Finally, the Church is dynamic and alive with the Spirit of God. The Holy Spirit has been given to the Church, and this same Spirit, as the soul of the Body of Christ (see *Lumen Gentium*, 7), moves its members, especially through the Sacraments, to Christlike holiness.

The second purpose of this document is to describe the mission of the Church, which is essentially a mission of unity and reconciliation. Just as the Holy Spirit rests within the Church to make its members holy, it also drives the members of the Body of Christ to continue the work of Christ. God's desire is to draw every person into unity and to share the very life of God with each person. This document on the Church describes God as a Father who has a single desire: to draw all people into his loving embrace. This is the reason he sent his Son, Jesus, and that is why Jesus established the Church. Acting as a sacrament of Christ, a sign and instrument of unity in Christ, the Church, being true to its nature and identity in the unity of the Holy Spirit, must work without ceasing to draw all people to the Father by proclaiming Jesus Christ as the way to the Father.

Note: This document and others in this book, according to the practice of previous times, uses the word *man* and *men* in a universal context to mean both men and women.

Excerpt from *Dogmatic Constitution on the Church (Lumen Gentium)*
By the Second Vatican Council

1. Christ is the Light of nations. Because this is so, this Sacred Synod gathered together in the Holy Spirit eagerly desires, by proclaiming the Gospel to every creature, (Cf. Mk. 16:15.) to bring the light of Christ to all men, a light brightly visible on the countenance of the Church. Since the Church is in Christ like a sacrament or as a sign and instrument both of a very closely knit union with God and of the unity of the whole human race, it desires now to unfold more fully to the faithful of the Church and to the whole world its own inner nature and universal mission.

2. The eternal Father, by a free and hidden plan of His own wisdom and goodness, created the whole world. His plan was to raise men to a participation of the divine life. Fallen in Adam, God the Father did not leave men to themselves, but ceaselessly offered helps to salvation, in view

Divine Life

There are many differing thoughts about what Heaven is. Although there is much to speculate about, one clear thing in the Church's teaching is that Heaven is entering into the life of God. Being united with Jesus means we enjoy that same relationship with God the Father that Jesus has through the power of the Holy Spirit. This will be a sharing of the divine life.

of Christ, the Redeemer "who is the image of the invisible God, the first-born of every creature." (Col. 1:15.) All the elect, before time began, the Father "foreknew and pre-destined to become conformed to the image of His Son, that he should be the firstborn among many brethren." (Rom. 8:29.) He planned to assemble in the holy Church all those who would believe in Christ. Already from the beginning of the world the foreshadowing of the Church took place. It was prepared in a remarkable way throughout the history of the people of Israel and by means of the Old Covenant. In the present era of time the Church was constituted and, by the outpouring of the Spirit, was made manifest. At the end of time it will gloriously achieve completion, when, as is read in the Fathers, all the just, from Adam and "from Abel, the just one, to the last of the elect,"[1] will be gathered together with the Father in the universal Church.

3. The Son, therefore, came, sent by the Father. It was in Him, before the foundation of the world, that the Father chose us and predestined us to become adopted sons, for in Him it pleased the Father to re-establish all things. (Cf. Eph. 1:4–5 and 10.) To carry out the will of the Father, Christ inaugurated the Kingdom of heaven on earth and revealed to us the mystery of that kingdom. By His obedience He brought about redemption. The Church, or, in other words, the kingdom of Christ now present in mystery, grows visibly through the power of God in the world. This inauguration and this growth are both symbolized by the blood and water which flowed from the open side of a crucified Jesus, (Cf. Jn. 19:34.) and are foretold in the words of the Lord referring to His death on the Cross: "And I, if I be lifted up from the earth, will draw all things to myself." (Jn. 12:32.) As often as the sacrifice of the cross in which Christ our Passover was sacrificed, (1 Cor. 5:7.) is celebrated on the altar, the work of our redemption is carried

on, and, in the sacrament of the eucharistic bread, the unity of all believers who form one body in Christ (Cf. 1 Cor. 10:17.) is both expressed and brought about. All men are called to this union with Christ, who is the light of the world, from whom we go forth, through whom we live, and toward whom our whole life strains.

4. When the work which the Father gave the Son to do on earth (Cf. Jn. 17:4.) was accomplished, the Holy Spirit was sent on the day of Pentecost in order that He might continually sanctify the Church, and thus, all those who believe would have

> *All men are called to this union with Christ, who is the light of the world, from whom we go forth, through whom we live, and toward whom our whole life strains.*

access through Christ in one Spirit to the Father. (Cf. Eph. 1:18.) He is the Spirit of Life, a fountain of water springing up to life eternal. (Cf. Jn. 4:14; 7:38–39.) To men, dead in sin, the Father gives life through Him, until, in Christ, He brings to life their mortal bodies. (Cf. Rom. 8:10–11.) The Spirit dwells in the Church and in the hearts of the faithful, as in a temple. (Cf. Cor. 3:16; 6:19.) In them He prays on their behalf and bears witness to the fact that they are adopted sons. (Cf. Gal. 4:6; Rom. 8:15–16 and 26.) The Church, which the Spirit guides in [the] way of all truth (Cf. Jn. 16:13.) and which He unified in communion and in works of ministry, He both equips and directs with **hierarchical** and **charismatic** gifts and adorns with His fruits. (Cf. Eph. 1:11–12; 1 Cor 12:4; Gal. 5:22.) By the power of the Gospel He makes the Church keep the freshness of youth. Uninterruptedly He renews it and leads it to perfect union with its Spouse. The Spirit and the Bride both say to Jesus, the Lord, "Come!" (Rev. 22:17.)

Thus, the Church has been seen as "a people made one with the unity of the Father, the Son and the Holy Spirit."[2]

hierarchical Related to the visible structure of service and teaching authority to the Body of Christ, with the bishops as shepherds and the Pope as the chief shepherd. Within this orderly structure, the Holy Spirit is active.

charismatic Referring to the gifts, or charisms, of the Holy Spirit that move all members of the Body of Christ.

5. The mystery of the holy Church is manifest in its very foundation. The Lord Jesus set it on its course by preaching the Good News, that is, the coming of the Kingdom of God, which, for centuries, had been promised in the Scriptures: "The time is fulfilled, and the kingdom of God is at hand" (Mk. 1:15; cf. Mt. 4:17.). In the word, in the works, and in the presence of Christ, this kingdom was clearly open to the view of men. . . .

When Jesus, who had suffered the death of the cross for mankind, had risen, He appeared as the one constituted as Lord, Christ and eternal Priest, (Cf. Acts 2:36; Heb. 5:6; 7:17–21.) and He poured out on His disciples the Spirit promised by the Father. (Cf. Acts 2:33.) From this source the Church, equipped with the gifts of its Founder and faithfully guarding His precepts of charity, humility and self-sacrifice, receives the mission to proclaim and to spread among all peoples the Kingdom of Christ and of God and to be, on earth, the initial budding forth of that kingdom. While it slowly grows, the Church strains toward the completed Kingdom and, with all its strength, hopes and desires to be united in glory with its King.

7. In the human nature united to Himself[,] the Son of God, by overcoming death through His own death and resurrection, redeemed man and re-molded him into a new creation. (Cf. Gal. 6:15; 2 Cor. 5:17.) By communicating His Spirit, Christ made His brothers, called together from all nations, mystically the components of His own Body.

In that Body the life of Christ is poured into the believers who, through the sacraments, are united in a hidden and real way to Christ who suffered and was glorified. Through Baptism we are formed in the likeness of Christ: "For in one Spirit we were all baptized into one body." (1 Cor. 12:13.) In this sacred rite a oneness with Christ's death and resurrection is both symbolized and brought about: "For we were buried with Him by means of Baptism into death"; and if "we have been united with Him in the likeness of His death, we shall be so in the likeness of His resurrection also." (Rom. 6:15.) Really partaking of the body of the Lord in the breaking of the Eucharistic bread, we are taken up into communion with Him and with one another. "Because the bread is one, we though many, are one body, all of us who partake of the one bread." (1 Cor. 10:17.) In this way all of us are made members of His Body, (Cf. 1 Cor 12:27.) "but severally members one of another." (Rom. 12:5.)

As all the members of the human body, though they are many, form one body, so also are the faithful in Christ. (Cf. 1 Cor 12:12.) Also, in the building up of Christ's Body various members and functions have their part to play. There is only one Spirit who, according to His own richness and the needs of the ministries, gives His different gifts for the welfare of the Church. (Cf. 1 Cor. 12:1–11.) What has a special place among these gifts is the grace of the apostles to whose authority the Spirit Himself subjected even those who were endowed with **charisms**. (Cf. 1 Cor 14.) Giving the body unity through Himself and through His power and inner joining of the members, this same Spirit produces and urges love among the believers. From all this it follows that if one member endures anything, all the members co-endure it, and if one member is honored, all the members together rejoice. (Cf. 1 Cor. 12:26.)

The Head of this Body is Christ. He is the image of the invisible God and in Him all things came into being. He is before all creatures and in Him all things hold together. He is the head of the Body which is the Church. He is the beginning, the firstborn from the dead, that in all things He might have the first place. (Cf. Col. 1:15–18.) By the greatness of His power He rules the things in heaven and the things on earth, and with His all-surpassing perfection and way of acting He fills the whole body with the riches of His glory.

All the members ought to be molded in the likeness of Him, until Christ be formed in them. (Cf. Gal. 4:19.) For this reason we, who have been made to conform with Him, who have died with Him and risen with Him, are taken up into the mysteries of His life, until we will reign together with Him. (Cf. Phil. 3:21; 2 Tim. 2:11; Eph. 2:6; Col. 2:12 etc.) On earth, still as pilgrims in a strange land, tracing in trial and in oppression the paths He trod, we are made one with His sufferings like the body is one with the Head, suffering with Him, that with Him we may be glorified. (Cf. Rom. 8:17.)

From Him "the whole body, supplied and built up by joints and ligaments,

> **charism** A special gift or grace of the Holy Spirit given to an individual Christian or community, commonly for the benefit and building up of the entire Church.

attains a growth that is of God." (Col. 2:19.) He continually distributes in His body, that is, in the Church, gifts of ministries in which, by His own power, we serve each other unto salvation so that, carrying out the truth in love, we might through all things grow unto Him who is our Head. (Cf. Eph. 4:11–16.)

In order that we might be unceasingly renewed in Him, (Cf. Eph. 4:23.) He has shared with us His Spirit who, existing as one and the same being in the Head and in the members, gives life to, unifies and moves through the whole body. This He does in such a way that His work could be compared by the holy Fathers with the function which the principle of life, that is, the soul, fulfills in the human body.

Christ loves the Church as His bride, having become the model of a man loving his wife as his body; (Cf. Eph. 5:25–28.) the Church, indeed, is subject to its Head. (Ibid. 23–24.) "Because in Him dwells all the fullness of the Godhead bodily." (Col. 2:9.) He fills the Church, which is His body and His fullness, with His divine gifts (Cf. Eph. 1:22–23.) so that it may expand and reach all the fullness of God. (Cf. Eph. 3:19.)

Endnotes

1. Cfr. S. Gregorius M., Hom in Evang. 19, 1: PL 76, 1154 B. S Augustinus, Serm. 341, 9, 11: PL 39, 1499 s. S. Io. Damascenus, Adv. Iconocl. 11: PG 96, 1357.
2. S. Cyprianus, De Orat Dom. 23: PL 4, 5S3, Hartel, III A, p. 28S. S. Augustinus, Serm. 71, 20, 33: PL 38, 463 s. S. Io. Damascenus, Adv. Iconocl. 12: PG 96, 1358 D.

For Reflection

1. After reading this excerpt from *Lumen Gentium,* how would you describe the Church's mission?

2. Describe, in your own words, the Body of Christ, the Church, and how we participate in it through the Sacraments.

3. The Church has the mission of drawing all people into unity. What do you think causes division within your community? What do you think you can do to break down those divisions?

3 The Sacraments: Encounters with Christ

Introduction

In the 1950s the world was changing. Two wars had just been fought on a global scale. Modern methods of communication meant that a free exchange of ideas was taking place among many different people from diverse cultures. People began to believe that scientific advancements could make space travel possible. University enrollments were increasing as more people, particularly in North America and Western Europe, sought educational opportunities. The dawn of the modern world was breaking, and the Christian faith was receiving renewed attention. At this same time, a group of young European theologians began to bring a new expression to the ancient Christian faith. The faith itself wasn't changing, but the world was.

Edward Schillebeeckx, OP (1914–2009), was among that group of young scholars. During these years he devoted much of his research, writings, and teaching to a theology of the Sacraments. In 1952, he completed his doctoral thesis, the major paper a student must complete to earn a doctor of philosophy degree. It explored the Sacraments and their role in salvation. Seven years later his book *Christ the Sacrament of the Encounter with God* was published. This book brought a fresh understanding to the Sacraments of the Catholic Church, and it helped to shape the sacramental theology and the theology of the Church later expressed during the Second Vatican Council. In his book Schillebeeckx outlines God's plan of salvation as originating in God the Father, then expressed in the Word of the Father, Jesus Christ, then from Christ to the Church, and from the Church to the Sacraments.

Schillebeeckx reasons in this way: God the Father wants to offer salvation to us, his people. Because human beings are bodily creatures, God's offer of salvation must be extended in visible, concrete ways. This is how Schillebeeckx defines a Sacrament: it is an offer of salvation that our bodies can perceive. Jesus is God's ultimate offer of salvation to us. For example, the people who heard Jesus' message and watched him heal both heard and saw the "sacrament" of God. Jesus, however, ascended into Heaven. Because he is in Heaven and no longer visible to us, how can our bodies receive God's offer of salvation? The visible invitation to salvation now comes through the Church. Christ is the sacrament of God, and the Church is the sacrament of Christ.

In the reading for this chapter, Schillebeeckx emphasizes the point that the Church is the Body of Christ, and he asks the reader to consider the full meaning of this term. The Body of Christ has individuals as members, and Jesus is the Head of that Body. Body and Head together constitute the "whole Christ." In the closing paragraph of the reading, Schillebeeckx writes, "To receive the sacraments of the Church in faith is therefore the same thing as to encounter Christ himself." The Church mediates physical encounters with the Risen Christ. This goes back to the original thought that human beings are bodily creatures. For a person to have any kind of encounter, it must be visible and perceptible to the body. For this reason, the Church is the sacrament of Christ.

Excerpt from *Christ the Sacrament of the Encounter with God*

By Edward Schillebeeckx

1. The Church, Earthly Sacrament of Christ in Heaven

We have said that Jesus as man and Messiah is unthinkable without his redemptive community. Established by God precisely in his vocation as representative of fallen mankind, Jesus had by his human life to win this community to himself and make of it a redeemed people of God. This means that Jesus the Messiah, through his death which the Father accepts, becomes in fact the head of the People of God, the Church assembled in his death. It is thus that he wins the Church to himself, by his **messianic** life as the Servant of God, as the fruit of the sufferings of his messianic sacrifice: "Christ dies that the Church might be born."[1] In his messianic sacrifice, which the Father accepts, Christ in his glorified body is himself the eschatological redemptive community of the Church. In his own self the glorified Christ is simultaneously "Head and members."

Eschatological Redemptive Community

Eschaton refers to the end times and the final act of salvation. The Church is the community of believers through whom the final act of salvation will come.

The earthly Church is the visible realization of this saving reality in history. The Church is a visible communion in grace. This communion itself, consisting of members and a hierarchical leadership, is the earthly sign of the triumphant redeeming grace of Christ. The fact must be emphasized that not only the hierarchical Church but also the community of the faithful belong to this grace-giving sign that is the Church. As much in its hierarchy as in the laity the community of the Church is the realization in historical form of the victory achieved by Christ. The inward communion in grace with God in Christ becomes visible in and is realized through the outward social sign. Thus the essence of the Church consists in this, that the final goal of grace achieved by Christ becomes visibly present in the whole Church as a visible society.

It was the custom in the past to distinguish between the soul of the Church (this would be the inward communion in grace with Christ) and the body of the Church (the visible society with its members and its authority). Only too rightly, this view has been abandoned. It was even, in a

messianic Referring to the Messiah. The people of Israel were waiting for the messiah, the "anointed one," to appear. The Messiah would come and save God's people. The Greek term for Messiah is *christos*. Jesus is the Christ and the Messiah because he is the Anointed One.

Priestly Hierarchy

The Church is hierarchical because it has an order of service and leadership from the Pope to the bishops to the priests. These servants and leaders are ordained to act as the person of Christ during sacramental celebrations.

sense, condemned by Pope Pius XII. The visible Church itself is the Lord's mystical body. The Church is the visible expression of Christ's grace and redemption, realized in the form of a society which is a sign (*societas signum*)[.] Any attempt to introduce a dualism here is the work of evil—as if one could play off the inward communion in grace with Christ against the juridical society of the Church, or vice versa. The Church therefore is not merely a means of salvation. It is Christ's salvation itself, this salvation as visibly realized in this world. Thus it is, by a kind of identity, the body of the Lord.

We remarked that this visibility of grace defines the whole Church; not the hierarchical Church only, but also the community of the faithful. The whole Church, the People of God led by a priestly hierarchy is "the sign raised up among the nations."[2] The activity, as much of the faithful as of their leaders, is thus an **ecclesial** activity.[3] This means that not only the hierarchy but also the believing people belong essentially to the **primordial sacrament** which is the earthly expression of this reality. As the sacramental Christ, the Church too is mystically both Head and members. When the twofold function of Christ becomes visible in the sign of the Christian community, it produces the distinction between hierarchy and faithful—a distinction of offices and of those who hold them. Even the hierarchy, on the one hand, are themselves part of the believing Church, and the faithful, on the other hand, share in the lordship of Christ and to some extent give it visibility, the sacramental functions of hierarchy and faithful differ within the Church and show the distinction.

ecclesial The Greek word *ekklesia* is best translated as "the gathering," "assembly," or "congregation." *Ecclesial* has come to mean "of or relating to a church."

primordial sacrament *Primordial* means "before time." In this sense *primordial sacrament* means the "original sacrament" or "the sacrament that is the source for all other sacraments."

4. A Sacrament: Official Act of the Church as Redemptive Institution

We are now in a position to draw up a definition of the sacramental action of the Church. A sacrament, that is an act of the primordial sacrament which is the Church, is a visible action proceeding from the Church as a redemptive institution, an official ecclesial act preformed in virtue either of the character of the priesthood or of the characters of baptism and confirmation. Hence in this sense a sacrament is actually something more than that which we usually understand under the term "seven sacraments," but it is also something more limited than that which we have just called "general visibility," meaning sacramentality as an outward manifestation not of office, but directly of inward communion in grace (i.e., the outwardly visible holiness of the life of the faithful in the Church). It is, however, necessary to assess the seven sacraments in their proper place within the wider sacramental context of the entire Church. A sacrament is primarily and fundamentally a personal act of Christ himself, which reaches and involves us in the form of an institutional act performed by a person in the Church who, in virtue of a sacramental character, is empowered to do so by Christ himself: an act *ex officio.* . . .

It follows from all we have said that these seven sacraments—before this or that particular one is specified—are all fundamentally and primarily a visible, official act of the Church.[4] Thus from the definition of the Church as the primordial sacrament, we come already to a first and general definition of the seven sacraments: Each sacrament is the personal saving act of the risen Christ himself, but realized in the visible form of an official act of the Church. In other words, a sacrament is the saving action of Christ in the visible form of an ecclesial action. The validity of a sacrament is therefore simply its authenticity as an act of the Church as such. The essential reality that in one

> **Each sacrament is the personal saving act of the risen Christ himself, but realized in the visible form of an official act of the Church.**

or other of seven possible ways is outwardly expressed in the reception of each of the sacraments is consequently the entry into living contact with the visible Church as the earthly mystery of Christ in heaven. To receive the sacraments of the Church in faith is therefore the same thing as to encounter Christ himself. In this light the sacramentality of the seven sacraments is the same as the sacramentality of the whole Church. This pervading "structure" of sacramentality is manifested by each of the seven sacraments in its own proper way.

Endnotes

1. "Moritur Christus ut fiat Ecclesia." (St. Augustine. In Evangelium Johannis. tract 9, 10 [PL, 35, col. 1463].)
2. Thus the Vatican Council. (DB, no. 1794.)
3. It is necessary for a clear presentation of the argument to adopt this form of the adjective. In everyday usage "ecclesiastical" has become so closely linked with all that concerns the hierarchical element in the Church; this currently more common word would therefore be misleading here and in the pages to follow, and circumlocution would not only prove cumbersome but also obscure the already compact text. "Ecclesial" is used to signify all that is proper to the Church in its entirety, a synthesis of hierarchical and lay elements (Translator.)[.]
4. It is not possible to set out every element implicit in our analysis. But it should be clear enough from all the subsequent discussion that seven sacraments, although primarily an official action of the hierarchical Church (through the minister), are not this alone, but also an official action of the recipient who, in virtue of his baptism, by the intention he expresses in the actual reception of the sacrament truly and coessentially contributes to the validity, the fully ecclesial realization, of the sacrament. This does not eliminate the differences specific to each individual sacrament (e.g., the special instances of the Eucharist, of matrimony, and of that sacrament which is the first to be received, baptism).

For Reflection

1. Schillebeeckx says that the Church is the visible sign of Christ. How have you seen the Church act as a visible sign of Christ to the world?

2. The reading speaks about the priestly hierarchy, but it also mentions the laity. How do you think you are called to be a visible sign of Christ to the world?

3. The first paragraph has the following quote: "Christ dies that the Church might be born." Considering everything you read in this chapter, how would you explain that quote?

4. After reading this chapter, how would you define the term *Sacrament*?

4 The Church as Sacrament

Introduction

What does it mean to say that the Church is a sacrament of Christ and so a missionary Church? This means that in every era the Church seeks to bring the Gospel, the Good News of Jesus Christ, to all people and to all nations. The Church exists for this very reason. Continuing the sacramental mission of Jesus Christ means that the Church is to be focused on outreach to the world that lies beyond the bounds of the Church. Despite this outward focus, it is also appropriate for the Church to take time to look within and seek deeper self-understanding. Such an examination is meant to make the Church more faithful and committed to her mission. The reading in this chapter is excerpted from a book written to help the Church to better understand her identity.

Avery Dulles, SJ (1918–2008), came from a family of famous and influential people. His father, his grandfather, and one of his great-uncles all served as U.S. secretaries of state. Washington Dulles International Airport, the airport that serves the Washington, D.C., area, was named for his father, John Foster Dulles.

Considering his family tree and his Harvard education, Avery Dulles, a convert to Catholicism in his early twenties, could have chosen a path of great worldly influence. Instead, after a year and a half at Harvard Law School and service in the U.S. Navy, he devoted himself to serving God as a priest in the Jesuit order. After earning a doctorate in sacred theology at the Gregorian University in Rome, Dulles became quite influential as a teacher and theologian and was eventually named a cardinal of the Church. He is especially remembered for his groundbreaking book *Models of Church*.

This book explores five valid, but different, ways or models of the Church: (1) Church as institution, (2) Church as mystical communion, (3) Church as sacrament, (4) Church as herald, and (5) Church as servant. The reading in this chapter is taken from the chapter "The Church as Sacrament." You will notice many similarities between this reading and the reading from Edward Schillebeeckx in chapter 3. Both describe Christ as the sacrament of God and the Church as the sacrament of Christ. Dulles examines this understanding of the Church as sacrament and completes the reflections on sacrament offered by Schillebeeckx. The Church is the sacrament of Christ to the world, but it is also a sacrament of the world to God. Just as Christ is the final and greatest offer of salvation from God, Christ is the final and greatest acceptance of God's offer of salvation. As a sacrament of Christ, the Church brings God's offer of salvation through Christ to the world, and it brings the world's acceptance of that offer through Christ to God.

Excerpt from *Models of the Church*
By Avery Dulles

The Church as Sacrament

As understood in the Christian tradition, sacraments are never merely individual transactions. Nobody baptizes, absolves, or anoints himself, and it is anomalous for the Eucharist to be celebrated in solitude. Here again the order of grace corresponds to the order of nature. Man comes into the world as a member of a family, a race, a people. He comes to maturity through encounter with his fellow men. Sacraments therefore have a dialogic structure. They take place in a mutual interaction that permits the people together to achieve a spiritual breakthrough that they could not achieve in isolation. A sacrament therefore is a socially constituted or communal symbol of the presence of grace coming to fulfillment.

On the basis of this general conception of sacrament we may now turn to two more specific theological notions: of Christ and of the Church as sacrament.

As Christians we believe that God is good and merciful, that he wills to communicate himself to man in spite of man's sinfulness and resistance to grace. We believe also that God's redemptive will is powerful and efficacious; that it therefore produces effects in history. God's grace is more powerful than man's sinfulness, so that when sin abounded, grace abounded even more (Rom. 5:20). Our belief in the superabundant power of grace when confronted by evil is founded upon the historical tangibility of God's redemptive love in Christ. Jesus Christ is the sacrament of God as turned toward man. He represents for us God's loving acceptance of man and his rehabilitation of man notwithstanding man's unworthiness.

> ## Christology from Below
>
> In this case, we can contrast "Christology from above" as being God's offering of salvation coming "down" to us from Christ. "Christology from below" describes our desire to be lifted "up" to God through Christ.

In characterizing Christ as God's sacrament, we are looking at Christ as he comes from above. But there is also, so to speak, a "Christology from below."[1] Grace impels men toward communion with God, and as grace works upon men it helps them to express what they are at a given stage in the process of redemption. Only in exteriorizing itself does grace achieve the highest intensity of its realization. Already in the Old Testament, Israel as a people constitutes a **sign** that historically expresses a real though imperfect yes-saying to God and no-saying to idolatry. Seen from below, Jesus belongs to this tangible history of salvation. As Servant of God he is the supreme sacrament of man's faithful response to God and of God's recognition of that fidelity. The entire history of grace has its summit and crown in Jesus Christ. He is simultaneously the sacrament of God's self-gift and of man's fully obedient acceptance. The mutual acceptance of God and man, initially signified by the history of Israel, reaches its consummation in Christ's cross and resurrection.

> **sign** In sacramental theology, *sign* has a unique meaning. It is a symbol of God's grace, but it also makes God's grace present. The Church is a symbol of people being united in Christ, but it also brings unity in Christ to reality.

Christ, as the sacrament of God, contains the grace that he signifies. Conversely, he signifies and confers the grace he contains. In him the invisible grace of God takes on visible form. But the sacrament of redemption is not complete in Jesus as a single individual. In order to become the kind of sign he must be, he must appear as the sign of God's redemptive love extended toward all mankind, and of the response of all mankind to that redemptive love.

The Church therefore is in the first instance a sign. It must signify in a historically tangible form the redeeming grace of Christ. It signifies that grace as relevantly given to men of every age, race, kind, and condition. Hence the Church must incarnate itself in every human culture.

The Church does not always signify this equally well. It stands under a divine imperative to make itself a convincing sign. It appears most fully as a sign when its members are evidently united to one another and to God through holiness and mutual love, and when they visibly gather to confess their faith in Christ and to celebrate what God has done for them in Christ.

As a sacrament the Church has both an outer and an inner aspect. The institutional or structural aspect of the Church—its external reality—is essential, since without it the Church would not be visible. Visible unity among all Christians is demanded, for without this the sign or communion that the Church is would be fragmented into a multitude of disconnected signs. It is thus of crucial importance that there should be manifest links of continuity among all the particular churches at any given time. Furthermore, it is important that the links should connect the Church of today with the Church of apostolic times. Otherwise the Church could not appear as the sign of our redemption in and through the historical Christ.

On the other hand, the institutional or structural aspect is never sufficient to constitute the Church. The offices and rituals of the Church must palpably appear as the actual expressions of the faith, hope, and love of living men. Otherwise the Church would be a dead body

> ### Institutional or Structural
>
> The Church has a visible organization and order. This structure must be enlivened with faith, hope, and love.

rather than a living Christian community. It would be an inauthentic sign—a sign of something not really present, and therefore not a sacrament.

But sacrament, as we have been saying, is a sign of grace realizing itself. Sacrament has an event character; it is dynamic. The Church becomes Church insofar as the grace of Christ, operative within it, achieves historical tangibility through the actions of the Church as such.

The Church becomes an actual event of grace when it appears most concretely as a sacrament—that is in the actions of the Church as such whereby men are bound together in grace by a visible expression. The more widely and intensely the faithful participate in this corporate action of the Church, the more the Church achieves itself.

In summary, the Church is not just a sign, but a sacrament. Considered as a bare institution, the Church might be characterized as just an empty sign. It could be going through formalities and be a hollow shell rather than a living community of grace.

But where the Church as sacrament is present, the grace of Christ will not be absent. That grace, seeking its appropriate form of expression—as grace inevitably does—will impel men to prayer, confession, worship, and other acts whereby the Church externally realizes its essence. Through these actions the Church signifies what it contains and contains what it signifies. In coming to expression the grace of the Church realizes itself as

> 66 *But where the Church as sacrament is present, the grace of Christ will not be absent.* 99

grace. The Church therefore confers the grace that it contains, and contains it precisely as conferring it. The Church becomes an event of grace as the lives of its members are transformed in hope, in joy, in self-forgetful love, in peace, in patience, and in all other Christlike virtues.

Endnote

1. See the article "Jesus Christ" in *Sacramentum Mundi*, Vol. 3 (New York: Herder & Herder, 1969), pp. 191–92 (Grillmeier), and pp. 197–98, 205–5 (Rahner).

For Reflection

1. Dulles says that when people interact with one another, they can achieve spiritual breakthroughs that they could not reach on their own. Do you agree with this statement? Why or why not?

2. The reading describes Christ as both the expression of God's self-gift to humanity and humanity's acceptance of God. How do you think this is reflected in the Sacraments?

3. The Church is to be visible to the world. That is why there is structure to the Church. But the Church could become a "dead body." What does Dulles mean by this?

4. Dulles wrote, "The Church becomes an event of grace as the lives of its members are transformed in hope, in joy, in self-forgetful love, in peace, in patience, and in all other Christlike virtues." As a member of the Church, how do you see grace acting in your life—in hope, joy, love, peace, patience and in other Christlike ways?

5 Sacraments and Liturgy

Introduction

Pope Saint John XXIII (1881–1963) convened the Second Vatican Council in 1962 to examine how the Church can best bring the Gospel to the modern world. In an ecumenical council, all of the bishops of the Church gathered together with theologians, scholars, and even leaders of other Christian communities to address this great challenge. Saint John XXIII believed that the message of Jesus Christ and the beauty of the Catholic Church could have a greater effect on the lives of men and women. With this charge the gathered leaders sought to bring a renewed understanding and interest in the Word of God, in the nature and mission of the Church, and in the sacred liturgy to people of the modern era.

The first document to emerge from the Second Vatican Council was *Dogmatic Constitution on the Sacred Liturgy* (*Sacrosanctum Concilium,* 1963). This groundbreaking document has provided the Church with a new understanding of all liturgical prayer, especially the Eucharistic liturgy. This chapter provides the most memorable parts of this important document. You will read that the Church recognizes that Christ is truly present at the Eucharistic liturgy in four ways: (1) in the sacred minister, the **priest,** (2) in the Church as it sings and prays, (3) in the reading of the Sacred Scripture, and (4) in the Eucharistic species. Before this document it was rare for the presence of Christ to be recognized in the liturgy in ways other

priest One who offers a sacrifice to God in worship. In the Catholic Church, one who has received the ministerial priesthood through the Sacrament of Holy Orders. The priest serves the community of faith by representing and assisting the bishop in teaching, governing, and presiding over the community's worship.

than in the Eucharistic species. You will also see that the Church proclaims that it is within the liturgy that our salvation is worked out, that the liturgy is the summit and the font of our faith, and that the liturgy is the action of all of the body of Christ and not limited to the priest alone. All of these points and new insights reach their fulfillment in the statement that the Church must ensure that the people gathered for worship will be fully conscious and actively involved in the worship of God in the liturgy. Before this document, people were urged to pray *at* Mass. Now they were being urged to pray *the* Mass. The Eucharistic liturgy, regardless of how beautifully presented, is not simply to be observed. It was given to the Church so that the people of God might participate with their whole being, offering themselves to Jesus and receiving the Body and Blood of Christ as his gift of life to them. Thus in this self-offering, the Body of Christ, the Church, would truly "live in Christ" and grow to be more like him.

Excerpt from *Dogmatic Constitution on the Sacred Liturgy (Sacrosanctum Concilium)*

By the Second Vatican Council

1. This sacred Council has several aims in view: it desires to impart an ever increasing vigor to the Christian life of the faithful; to adapt more suitably to the needs of our own times those institutions which are subject to change; to foster whatever can promote union among all who believe in Christ; to strengthen whatever can help to call the whole of mankind into the household of the Church. The Council therefore sees particularly cogent reasons for undertaking the reform and promotion of the liturgy.

2. For the liturgy, "through which the work of our redemption is accomplished,"[1] most of all in the divine sacrifice of the Eucharist, is the outstanding means whereby the faithful may express in their lives, and manifest to others, the mystery of Christ and the real nature of the true Church. It is of the essence of the Church that she be both human and divine, visible and yet invisibly equipped, eager to act and yet intent on

contemplation, present in this world and yet not at home in it; and she is all these things in such wise that in her the human is directed and subordinated to the divine, the visible likewise to the invisible, action to contemplation, and this present world to that city yet to come,

which we seek [Cf. Heb. 13:14]. While the liturgy daily builds up those who are within into a holy temple of the Lord, into a dwelling place for God in the Spirit [Cf. Eph. 2:21–22], to the mature measure of the fullness of Christ [Cf. Eph. 4:13], at the same time it marvelously strengthens their power to preach Christ, and thus shows forth the Church to those who are outside as a sign lifted up among the nations [Cf. Is. 11:12] under which the scattered children of God may be gathered together [Cf. John 11:52], until there is one sheepfold and one shepherd [Cf. John 10:16]. . . .

7. To accomplish so great a work, Christ is always present in His Church, especially in her liturgical celebrations. He is present in the sacrifice of the Mass, not only in the person of His minister, "the same now offering, through the ministry of priests, who formerly offered himself on the cross,"[2] but especially under the Eucharistic species. By His power He is present in the sacraments, so that when a man baptizes it is really Christ Himself who baptizes.[3] He is present in His word, since it is He Himself who speaks when the holy scriptures are read in the Church. He is present, lastly, when the Church prays and sings, for He promised: "Where two or three are gathered together in my name, there am I in the midst of them" (Matt. 18:20).

Christ indeed always associates the Church with Himself in this great work wherein God is perfectly glorified and men are sanctified. The Church is His beloved Bride who calls to her Lord, and through Him offers worship to the Eternal Father.

**Four Ways
Christ Is Present**

Christ is truly present at the Eucharistic liturgy in four ways: (1) the prayers and singing, (2) the Scriptures, (3) the priest, and (4) especially the Eucharistic species.

Rightly, then, the liturgy is considered as an exercise of the priestly office of Jesus Christ. In the liturgy the **sanctification** of the man is signified by signs perceptible to the senses, and is effected in a way which corresponds with each of these signs; in the liturgy the whole public worship is performed by the Mystical Body of Jesus Christ, that is, by the Head and His members.

From this it follows that every liturgical celebration, because it is an action of Christ the priest and of His Body which is the Church, is a sacred action surpassing all others; no other action of the Church can equal its efficacy by the same title and to the same degree. . . .

10. . . . The liturgy is the summit toward which the activity of the Church is directed; at the same time it is the font from which all her power flows. For the aim and object of apostolic works is that all who are made sons of God by faith and baptism should come together to praise God in the midst of His Church, to take part in the sacrifice, and to eat the Lord's supper.

The liturgy in its turn moves the faithful, filled with "the paschal sacraments," to be "one in holiness"[4]; it prays that "they may hold fast in their lives to what they have grasped by their faith"[5]; the renewal in the Eucharist of the covenant between the Lord and man draws the faithful into the compelling love of Christ and sets them on fire. From the liturgy, therefore, and especially from the Eucharist, as from a font, grace is poured forth upon us; and the sanctification of men in Christ and the glorification of God, to which all other activities of the Church are directed as toward their end, is achieved in the most efficacious possible way.

sanctification From *sanctify*, meaning "to set apart or make holy." Those who are sanctified are set apart because they more closely imitate the ways of Christ. Sanctification is the process of becoming closer to God and growing in holiness, taking on the righteousness of Jesus Christ with the gift of sanctifying grace.

11. But in order that the liturgy may be able to produce its full effects, it is necessary that the faithful come to it with proper dispositions, that

their minds should be attuned to their voices, and that they should cooperate with divine grace lest they receive it in vain [Cf. 2 Cor. 6:1]. Pastors of souls must therefore realize that, when the liturgy is celebrated, something more is required than the mere observation of the laws governing valid and licit celebration; it is their duty also to ensure that the faithful take part fully aware of what they are doing, actively engaged in the rite, and enriched by its effects.

> 66 *But in order that the liturgy may be able to produce its full effects, it is necessary that the faithful come to it with proper dispositions, that their minds should be attuned to their voices, and that they should cooperate with divine grace lest they receive it in vain.* 99

12. The spiritual life, however, is not limited solely to participation in the liturgy. The Christian is indeed called to pray with his brethren, but he must also enter into his chamber to pray to the Father, in secret [Cf. Matt. 6:6]; yet more, according to the teaching of the Apostle, he should pray without ceasing [Cf. 1 Thess. 5:17]. We learn from the same Apostle that we must always bear about in our body the dying of Jesus, so that the life also of Jesus may be made manifest in our bodily frame [Cf. 2 Cor. 4:10–11]. This is why we ask the Lord in the sacrifice of the Mass that, "receiving the offering of the spiritual victim," he may fashion us for himself "as an eternal gift."[6] . . .

14. Mother Church earnestly desires that all the faithful should be led to that fully conscious, and active participation in liturgical celebrations which is demanded by the very nature of the liturgy. Such participation by the Christian people as "a chosen race, a royal priesthood, a holy nation, a redeemed people" (1 Pet. 2:9; cf. 2:4–5), is their right and duty by reason of their baptism.

Fully Conscious and Active

In this document, we read that people gathered at the Eucharist are to give themselves completely to the liturgy. Their hearts, their minds, and their bodies are to be focused, without reservation, on the act of worship in the liturgy. Ensuring such participation is the principal concern of all liturgical renewal and activity.

In the restoration and promotion of the sacred liturgy, this full and active participation by all the people is the aim to be considered before all else; for it is the primary and indispensable source from which the faithful are to derive the true Christian spirit; and therefore pastors of souls must zealously strive to achieve it, by means of the necessary instruction, in all their pastoral work.

Endnotes

1. Secret of the ninth Sunday after Pentecost.
2. Council of Trent, Session XXII, Doctrine on the Holy Sacrifice of the Mass, c. 2.
3. Cf. St. Augustine, Tractatus in Ioannem, VI, n. 7.
4. Postcommunion for both Masses of Easter Sunday.
5. Collect of the Mass for Tuesday of Easter Week.
6. Secret for Monday of Pentecost Week.

For Reflection

1. Please explain how you see the liturgy as the source of the Church's activity and the summit of the Church's life.

2. The reading says that Christ is always with the Church, especially in the liturgy. How does the liturgy help you to bring Christ to others outside the liturgy?

3. *Sacrosanctum Concilium* reminds us that the people of God should come to the liturgy "with proper dispositions, that their minds should be attuned to their voices, and that they should cooperate with divine grace lest they receive it in vain." Name three ways you can best prepare for the liturgy and participate in it.

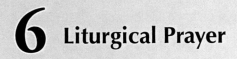

6 Liturgical Prayer

Introduction

Pope Emeritus Benedict XVI can be described as a living history of the Church. He has had a front-row seat to the major Church and world events of the mid-twentieth and early twenty-first centuries. He was a boy in Germany during World War II, an assistant at the Second Vatican Council, an archbishop and cardinal during the 1970s through the 1990s, and finally was elected Pope in 2005. He resigned his office as Pope in 2013 for reasons of health. In the introduction to chapter 3, we mentioned the young theologians who were bringing a new expression and a new understanding of the Christian faith in the 1950s. The young Joseph Ratzinger, the man who became Pope Benedict XVI, was among that group of theologians.

In his years as a theologian and author, he provided the Church with writings on a wide range of topics. Even as Pope, he continued to write and publish books on theological and spiritual themes. His longest-lasting effect on the Church might be on the way that Roman Catholics celebrate the liturgy of the Eucharist, the Mass. His book *The Spirit of the Liturgy* was influential in the way that we both understand and celebrate the liturgy. The reading in this chapter describes the relationship between time and space in the liturgy.

Essentially, Ratzinger explains that there is neither time nor space in the liturgy. The liturgy is the event that brings Heaven together with earth and unites them into a single moment. Those who gather at the liturgy are made "contemporary with the Paschal Mystery of Christ." The Eucharistic elements are the Body and Blood of Christ under the appearances of bread and wine.

However, Ratzinger is inviting the reader to think in another way. The Son of God joins us, and he is made real in our time and in our churches or school, but we are also lifted up into union with him. Jesus said yes to the Father's will for his life. The liturgy takes us from our present moment and brings us to the crucial moment of Jesus' yes to the Father. In the liturgy we can be united with Jesus, and our yes to the Father is joined with Jesus' yes to the Father.

Excerpt from *The Spirit of the Liturgy*
By Joseph Ratzinger (Pope Emeritus Benedict XVI)

The Relationship of the Liturgy to Time and Space: Some Preliminary Questions

> **Cosmic Liturgy**
>
> When the liturgy is celebrated, it is an event that all of creation participates in. It is not bound by the time and the location where it is being celebrated.

Can there really be special holy places and holy times in the world of Christian faith? Christian worship is surely a cosmic liturgy, which embraces both heaven and earth. The epistle to the Hebrews stresses that Christ suffered "outside the gate" and adds this exhortation: "Therefore let us go forth to him outside the camp, bearing abuse for him" (13:12). Is the whole world not now his sanctuary? Is sanctity not to be practiced by living one's daily life in the right way? Is our divine worship not a matter of being loving people in our daily life? Is *that* not how we become like God and so draw near to the true sacrifice? Can the **sacral** be anything other than imitating Christ in the simple patience of daily life? Can there be any other holy time than the time for practicing love of neighbor, whenever and wherever the circumstances of our life demand it?

Whoever asks questions like these touches on a crucial dimension of the Christian understanding of worship, but overlooks something essential about

sacral From *sacred*, this word describes rituals related to worship and other activities of prayer.

the permanent limits of the "not yet" that is part of the Christian existence and talks as if the New Heaven and New Earth had already come.

The Christ-event and the growth of the Church out of all the nations, the transition from Temple sacrifice to universal worship "in spirit and truth," is the first important step across the frontier, a step toward the fulfillment of the promises of the Old Testament. But it is obvious that hope

has not yet fully attained its goal. The New Jerusalem needs no Temple because Almighty God and the Lamb are themselves its Temple. In this City, instead of sun and moon, it is the glory of God and its lamp, the Lamb, that shed their brilliance (cf. Rev 21:22f.). But this City is not yet here. That is why the Church Fathers described the various stages of fulfillment, not just as a contrast between Old and New Testaments, but as the three steps of shadow, image, and reality. In the Church of the New Testament the shadow has been scattered by the image: "The night is far gone, the day is at hand" (Rom 13:12). But, as St. Gregory the Great puts it, it is still only the time of dawn, when darkness and light are intermingled. The sun is rising, but it has still not reached its zenith. Thus the time of the New Testament is a peculiar kind of "in-between," a mixture of "already and not yet." The empirical conditions of life in this world are still in force, but they have been burst open, and must be more and more burst open, in preparation for the final fulfillment already inaugurated in Christ.

This idea of the New Testament as the between-time, as image between shadow and reality, gives liturgical theology its specific form. It becomes even clearer when we bear in mind the three levels on which Christian worship operates, the three levels that make it what it is. There is the middle level, the strictly liturgical level, which is familiar to us all and is revealed in the words and actions of Jesus at the Last Supper. These words and actions form the core of Christian liturgical celebration, which was further constructed out of the synthesis of the synagogue and Temple liturgies. The sacrificial actions of the Temple have been replaced by the Eucharistic Prayer, which enters into what Jesus did at the Last Supper, and by the distribution of consecrated gifts. But this properly liturgical level does not stand on its own. It has meaning only in relation to something that really happens, to a reality that is substantially present. Otherwise it would lack real content, like bank notes without funds to cover them. The Lord could say that his Body was "given" only because he *had* in fact given it; he could present his Blood in the new chalice as shed for many only because he really *had* shed it. This Body is not the ever-dead corpse of a dead man, nor is the Blood the life-element rendered lifeless. No, sacrifice has become gift, for the Body given in love and the Blood given in love have entered, through the Resurrection, into the eternity of love, which is stronger than death. Without the Cross and Resurrection, Christian worship is null and void, and a theology of liturgy that omitted any reference to them would really just be talking about an empty game.

In considering this foundation of reality that undergirds Christian liturgy, we need to take account of another important matter. The Crucifixion of Christ, his death on the Cross, and, in another way, the act of his Resurrection from the grave, which bestows incorruptibility on the corruptible, are historical events that happen just once and as such belong to the past. The word *semel (ephapax)*, "once for all," which the epistle to the Hebrews emphasizes so vigorously in contrast to the multitude of repeated sacrifices in the Old Covenant, is strictly applicable to them. But if they were no more than facts in the past, like all the dates we learn in history books, then there could be nothing contemporary about them. In the end they would remain beyond our reach. However, the exterior act of being crucified is accompanied by an interior act of self-giving (the Body is "given for you"). "No one takes [my life] from me," says the Lord in St. John's Gospel, "but I lay it down of my own accord"(10:18). This act of giving is in no way just a spiritual occurrence. It is a spiritual act that takes up the bodily into itself, that embraces the whole man; indeed, it is at the same time an act of the Son. As St. Maximus the Confessor showed so splendidly, the obedience of Jesus' human will is inserted into the everlasting Yes of the Son to the Father. This "giving" on the part of the Lord, in the passivity of his being crucified, draws the passion of human existence into the action of love, and so it embraces all the dimensions of reality—Body, Soul, Spirit, Logos. Just as the pain of the body is drawn into the **pathos** of the mind and becomes the Yes of obedience, so time is drawn into what reaches beyond time. The real interior act, though it does not exist without the exterior, transcends time, but since it comes from time, time can again and again be brought into it. That is how we can become contemporary with the past events of salvation. St. Bernard of Clairvaux has this in mind when he says that the true *semel* ("once") bears within itself the *semper* ("always"). What is perpetual takes place in what happens only once. In the Bible the Once for All is emphasized most vigorously in the epistle to the Hebrews, but the careful reader will discover that the point made by St. Bernard expresses its true meaning. The *ephapax* ("Once For All") is bound up with the *aiōnios* ("everlasting"). "Today" embraces the whole time of the Church. And so in the Christian liturgy we not only receive something from the past but become

> 66 *In the Eucharist we are caught up and made contemporary with the Paschal Mystery of Christ in his passing from the tabernacle of the transitory to the presence and sight of God.* 99

contemporaries with what lies at the foundation of that liturgy. Here is the real heart and true grandeur of the celebration of the Eucharist, which is more, much more than a meal. In the Eucharist we are caught up and made contemporary with the Paschal Mystery of Christ in his passing from the tabernacle of the transitory to the presence and sight of God.

pathos A Greek word meaning "suffering"; also feelings of empathy for someone who is sad or suffering.

For Reflection

1. Explain what Ratzinger means when he uses the terms *in-between* and *already and not yet*.

2. Some people have said that we leave our time and enter into God's time at the liturgy. What do you think is meant by this?

3. Ratzinger mentions Jesus' yes. How would you describe Jesus' yes?

4. How does the Eucharist unite us to the Paschal Mystery of Christ?

7 The Liturgy and Personal Prayer

Introduction

Saint Catherine of Siena (1347–1380) is one of three women who have been given the title Doctor of the Church. (The other two are Saints Teresa of Ávila and Thérèse of Lisieux.) The Church gives this title to those whose teachings have had a long-lasting, significant effect on the life of the Church. Catherine's influence spanned politics, the papacy, and mystical prayer. During her lifetime, controversy over the papacy was continual and damaging to people of faith. The great controversy erupted when the Pope, the Bishop of Rome, responded to political pressure and fled the city to live in Avignon, France. After six popes had lived in Avignon, Catherine wrote reverently, yet directly, to Pope Gregory XI and urged him to come back to Rome, which he eventually did.

The confidence that she showed in being able to speak frankly with the Pope came from her understanding of who she was and the person she was called to be by God. In this chapter we have a message that was written by a secretary as Catherine spoke. At that time Catherine was in ecstasy, or intense union with God. While in ecstasy she spoke her message from God directly; that is, the "first person" ("I" or "Me") was God speaking through her. In this message, insights into Catherine's prayer, her relationship with herself, and her relationship with God are revealed.

Communion with God is the overall theme of this particular message. Catherine mentions the sacramental communion that happens when we eat the Body and drink the Blood of Christ. She also mentions a type of communion that happens through authentic prayer. You will notice she distinguishes between vocal prayer and mental prayer. She does not want to do away with vocal prayer, such as the Lord's Prayer, the Hail Mary, or devotional prayers. However, she notes that for personal prayer to end in deep communion with God, it must go deeper within the person to mental prayer. It is in mental prayer that we come to knowledge of who God is and knowledge of who we are. She places a great value on self-knowledge and true humility. Self-knowledge lies in understanding our actions and motives, and humility lies in knowing God's mercy, his love, and his acceptance. Through the practice of mental prayer and from an understanding of God's relationship with us, we are better able to enter into sacramental communion and into communion with God through personal prayer.

Note: In the following excerpt, she is used to refer not to Catherine alone, but to the soul of the human being.

Excerpt from *Dialogues*
By Saint Catherine of Siena

"Know, dearest daughter, how, by humble, continual, and faithful prayer, the soul acquires, with time and perseverance, every virtue.

"Wherefore should she persevere and never abandon prayer, either through the illusion of the Devil or her own fragility, that is to say, either on account of any thought or movement coming from her own body, or of the words of any creature. The Devil often places himself upon the tongues of creatures, causing them to chatter nonsensically, with the purpose of preventing the prayer of the soul. All of this she should pass by, by means of the virtue of perseverance.

"Oh, how sweet and pleasant to that soul and to Me is holy prayer, made in the house of knowledge of self and of Me, opening the eye of the intellect to the light of faith, and the affections to the abundance of My charity, which was made visible to you, through My visible only-begotten Son, who showed it to you with His blood! Which Blood inebriates the soul and clothes her with the fire of divine charity, giving her the food of the Sacrament [which is placed in the **tavern** of the mystical body of the Holy Church] that is to say, the food of the Body and Blood of My

Son, wholly God and wholly man, administered to you by the hand of My vicar, who holds the key of the Blood.

"This is that tavern, which I mentioned to you, standing on the Bridge, to provide food and comfort for the travelers and the pilgrims, who pass by the way of the doctrine of My Truth, lest they should faint

through weakness. This food strengthens little or much, according to the desire of the recipient, whether he receives sacramentally or virtually.

"He receives sacramentally when he actually communicates with the Blessed Sacrament. He receives virtually when he communicates, both by desire of communion, and by contemplation of the Blood of Christ crucified, communicating, as it were, sacramentally, with the affection of love, which is to be tasted in the Blood which, as the soul sees, was shed through love. On seeing this the soul becomes inebriated, and blazes with holy desire and satisfies herself, becoming full of love for Me and for her neighbor.

"Where can this be acquired?

"In the house of self-knowledge with holy prayer, where imperfections are lost, even as Peter and the disciples, while they remained in watching and prayer, lost their imperfection and acquired perfection. By what means is this acquired? By perseverance seasoned with the most holy faith.

"But do not think that the soul receives such ardor and nourishment from prayer, if she pray only vocally, as do many souls whose prayers are rather words than love. Such as these give heed to nothing except to completing Psalms and saying many **paternosters**. And when they have once completed their

tavern Taken from the Latin word *taberna*, it means "hut" or "shop." In Catherine's time, it referred to places where travelers would stop for rest and refreshment along their way.

paternoster The Latin word for "our father." Catherine is referring to the Lord's Prayer.

Mental Prayer

Saint Catherine teaches that the whole person should be engaged in prayer. While the words of a prayer are being spoken, the mind and heart should actively seek to be in union with God.

appointed tale, they do not appear to think of anything further, but seem to place devout attention and love in merely vocal recitation, which the soul is not required to do, for, in doing only this, she bears but little fruit, which pleases Me but little.

"But if you ask Me, whether the soul should abandon vocal prayer, since it does not seem to all that they are called to mental prayer, I should reply 'No.' The soul should advance by degrees, and I know well that, just as the soul is at first imperfect and afterwards perfect, so also is it with her prayer. She should nevertheless continue in vocal prayer, while she is yet imperfect, so as not to fall into idleness. But she should not say her vocal prayers without joining them to mental prayer, that is to say, that while she is reciting, she should endeavor to elevate her mind in My love, with the consideration of her own defects and of the Blood of My only-begotten Son, wherein she finds the breadth of My charity and the remission of her sins.

"And this she should do, so that self-knowledge and the consideration of her own defects should make her recognize My goodness in herself and continue her exercises with true humility. I do not wish defects to be considered in particular, but in general, so that the mind may not be contaminated by the remembrance of particular and hideous sins. But, as I said, I do not wish the soul to consider her sins, either in general or in particular, without also remembering the Blood and the broadness of My mercy, for fear that otherwise she should be brought to confusion.

"And together with confusion would come the Devil, who has caused it, under color of contrition and displeasure of sin, and so she would arrive at eternal damnation, not only on account of her confusion, but also through the despair which would come to her, because she did not seize the arm of My mercy. This is one of the subtle devices with which the Devil deludes My servants, and, in order to escape from his deceit, and to be pleasing to Me, you must enlarge your hearts and affections in My boundless mercy, with true humility.

"And so, with exercise in perseverance, she will taste prayer in truth, and the food of the Blood of My only-begotten Son, and therefore I told you that some communicated virtually with the Body and Blood of Christ, although not sacramentally; that is, they communicate in the affection of charity, which they taste by means of holy prayer, little or much, according to the affection with which they pray. They who proceed with little prudence and without method, taste little, and they who proceed with much, taste much.

"For the more the soul tries to loosen her affection from herself, and fasten it in Me with the light of the intellect, the more she knows; and the more she knows, the more she loves, and, loving much, she tastes much. You see then, that perfect prayer is not attained to through many words, but through affection of desire, the soul raising herself to Me, with knowledge of herself and of My mercy, seasoned the one with the other. Thus she will exercise together mental and vocal prayer, for, even as the active and contemplative life is one, so are they. . . .

"Each one, according to his condition, ought to exert himself for the salvation of souls, for this exercise lies at the root of a holy will, and whatever he may contribute, by words or deeds, towards the salvation of his neighbor, is virtually a prayer, although it does not replace a prayer which one should make oneself at the appointed season, as My glorious standard-bearer Paul said, in the words, 'He who ceases not to work ceases not to pray.'

"It was for this reason that I told you that prayer was made in many ways, that is, that actual prayer may be united with mental prayer if made with the affection of charity, which charity is itself continual prayer. I have now told you how mental prayer is reached by exercise and perseverance, and by leaving vocal prayer for mental when I visit the soul. I have also spoken to you of common prayer, that is, of vocal prayer in general, made outside of ordained times, and of the prayers of good-will, and how every exercise, whether performed in oneself or in one's neighbor, with good-will, is prayer."

or Reflection

1. How would you describe the distinction between vocal prayer and mental prayer?

2. Why do you think Catherine places such a high value on self-knowledge?

3. Why do you think it is dangerous to think about one's sinfulness without also keeping God's mercy in mind?

4. Catherine writes that "every exercise" (action) performed with good-will is prayer. What does she mean by this? How do you think this can be relevant for your life?

Part 2
The Sacraments of Christian Initiation

8 Christian Initiation: The Beginning of Christian Life

Introduction

"What must I do to be saved?" (Acts of the Apostles 16:30) This question reveals something common in our experience of being human. We desire deliverance, freedom, and **salvation**. The Christian believer has found the answer to this desire and this question in the person of Jesus Christ. The Son of God, Jesus, the Christ, reveals God to us, because Jesus is truly God. He also reveals ourselves to us, because he is truly human. He shows us what a true human being should be.

The Church teaches that we have been created to be in an intimate relationship with God. In fact there is a constant restlessness or desire inside each person for such a relationship with the Father. Saint Augustine wrote in *Confessions:* "You have made us for yourself, and our hearts are restless until they find rest in you" (Book I, Chapter 1*)*. It is a desire that we can actually feel as we live life. Jesus Christ is the perfect human who has always lived in complete intimacy with God. As humans join their lives to Jesus' life, they fulfill their calling and their longing for intimacy with God. The Church teaches that we enter into this rela-

salvation From the Latin *salvare*, meaning "to save," referring to the forgiveness of sins and the restoration of friendship with God, attained for us through the Paschal Mystery—Christ's work of redemption accomplished through his Passion, death, Resurrection, and Ascension. Only at the time of judgment can a person be certain of salvation, which is a gift of God.

Sacraments of Christian Initiation The three Sacraments—Baptism, Confirmation, and the Eucharist—through which we enter into full membership in the Church.

tionship through the **Sacraments of Christian Initiation**—Baptism, Confirmation, and the Eucharist. We are brought into communion with the Father because he has adopted us as his daughters and sons.

When we are adopted into God, we are not alone. Our relationship is not with the Father, Jesus, and the Holy Spirit alone. Rather, we are brought into God's family, the Body of Christ. Christians are never alone. As we learned in reading our first selection from *Dogmatic Constitution on the Church (Lumen Gentium)* in chapter 2, the initiated Christian is one member of the Church, the Body of Christ—one member among many people. This is why community is important. When we are in an intimate relationship with God, we are in intimate relationships with believers throughout the world and through the centuries. In this chapter's short selection from *Lumen Gentium,* note that this membership in the one Body of Christ leads to unity with him and with one another through the Sacraments of Baptism, Confirmation, and the Eucharist. In our second reading, "Christian Initiation: Gate to Salvation," Monika Hellwig describes the power of community, and she challenges us to become a true community that calls people to holiness. If we initiate people into our community, Hellwig asks, are we a community that forms people into the image of Jesus? Finally, Aidan Kavanaugh describes the initiation of a young boy in the fourth century. This transforming encounter leaves no doubt that the initiation experience joins us with Jesus Christ. It joins us in intimacy with God and with the members of the Body of Christ.

Excerpt from *Dogmatic Constitution on the Church (Lumen Gentium)*
By the Second Vatican Council

11. It is through the sacraments and the exercise of the virtues that the sacred nature and organic structure of the priestly community is brought into operation. Incorporated in the Church through baptism, the faithful

are destined by the baptismal character for the worship of the Christian religion; reborn as sons of God they must confess before men the faith which they have received from God through the Church. They are more perfectly bound to the Church by the sacrament of Confirmation, and the Holy Spirit endows them with special strength so that they are more strictly obliged to spread and defend the faith, both by word and by deed, as true witnesses of Christ. Taking part in the Eucharistic sacrifice, which is the fount and apex of the whole Christian life, they offer the Divine Victim to God, and offer themselves along with It. Thus both by reason of the offering and through Holy Communion all take part in this liturgical service, not indeed, all in the same way but each in that way which is proper to himself. Strengthened in Holy Communion by the Body of Christ, they then manifest in a concrete way that unity of the people of God which is suitably signified and wondrously brought about by this most august sacrament.

Excerpt from "Christian Initiation: Gate to Salvation"

By Monika Hellwig

Sin is essentially disorientation, alienation from God, from others and from one's true, peaceful self. Salvation then is by a turning, a re-orientation to God, to community with others, to peace with oneself—a re-orientation of the individual and a re-orientation of society in its community concerns and relationships and also in its structures large and small. And this is why baptism is the sacrament of the great turning; it is the return to community with others in the context of a turning of one's life to God and to God's purpose in the world and in history, and that is a return to one's true self, to the truth of one's self as creature before the creator and among other creatures. Baptism assumes not only the candidate's appreciation of what is at stake and the candidate's readiness to be brought to this turning. It also assumes a community to which the candidate can return—a community that is in some sense already that of the final reconciliation. The turning is in the last resort a community as well as a personal matter.

The **redemption** which Christians have experienced in Jesus Christ is a restoration of the focus and integration and therefore the joy and the purpose of human existence. What was restored in the person of Jesus himself is shared with all who can be drawn into relationship with him. Because sin is essentially the state of disorientation and alienation, therefore salvation is essentially a matter of re-orientation and of reconciliation. It is re-orientation to God and that brings all else into perspective. It is reconciliation with God and that is worked out in some very specific and concrete reconciliations within creation. The very existence of Jesus in the world, in history, gives a new center to human existence—a center around which others, individually and in their social groupings and structures, can come together to become whole, to become authentically themselves as created by God, and therefore to find fulfillment and peace.

> 66 *Baptism is the sacrament of the great turning; it is the return to community with others in the context of a turning of one's life to God and to God's purpose in the world and in history, and that is a return to one's true self, to the truth of one's self as creature before the creator and among other creatures.* 99

However, this re-integration of all human life in Jesus is made possible by the mediation of those who extend the presence of Jesus to one another across great stretches of space and time and cultural variations. It is a community of followers of Jesus, themselves transformed in his Spirit alive in them, that is able to forge links through space and time and culture that channel the grace of Christ to others to transform their lives in turn. That quality of life, that open relationship with God and with God's good creation, which we call grace because it is wholly gift, does not drop into human hearts directly from heaven and is not "produced" by the performance of a ritual. Like

redemption From the Latin *redemptio*, meaning "a buying back"; referring, in the Old Testament, to Yahweh's deliverance of Israel and, in the New Testament, to Christ's deliverance of all Christians from the forces of sin.

all human relationships, and qualities and values, grace is communicated through the encounter with graced and gracious persons. And this grace is salvation in process.

Baptism and confirmation and first eucharistic communion, therefore, making up the process of Christian initiation, are sacramental and effective in this truly divine and truly human way. Sacraments give body to spiritual reality, specificity to what is otherwise diffused, visibility and palpability to what is otherwise elusive. The ritual gives expression and concreteness to the transition from a life of chaos and frustration to a life of reconciliation, purpose and communion. The ritual cannot substitute for this transition; it is intended to facilitate it and thereby mediate or confer grace. . . .

When we claim that the initiation into the Christian community is a gateway to salvation, young people come with certain felt needs for salvation, certain deprivations, fears and sufferings from which they know they need to be rescued, certain perceptions of what is wrong and unjust in the world which they know must be changed. They want to know whether the salvation the Church offers has anything to say to the real problems which they perceive. What is even more important, perhaps, is that they have a right to come with these questions and their demands are in keeping with the true nature of the sacraments of initiation and the true nature of the Church.

The specific fears that haunt young people of our times and from which they want to be redeemed are important. There is the never wholly absent fear of nuclear holocaust which constitutes a pervasive threat to the future of the human race. There is fear of being excluded in the fierce economic competition—a fear of joblessness, of incompetence, of failure, of being overwhelmed, of being unvalued and unwanted in the marketplace. There is also the fear of personal loneliness and isolation, of being left out, of being despised for nonconformity to the peer group expectations, of being ridiculed or made the butt of prejudice, of not being acceptable for what one is. There is also the fear of violence in our society, of the cold selfishness of others, of infidelity in marriages and families, and of the instability and vulnerability which spring from family infidelity. Moreover, there is often a realization among the young of the huge intractable problems of racial prejudice, oppression of the poor and powerless masses, corruption in public life, warmongering for financial profit and so forth.

The young people whom we have baptized in infancy and whom we are inviting to full and adult membership in our Christian communities want to know and have a right to know whether the salvation we claim to offer has any "cash value" in the world of these problems and fears that threaten and overwhelm them. If we are honest, we do not pressure them to complete their initiation in confirmation and solemn first eucharistic communion . . . unless and until they themselves are convinced that they have found the answer to their questions, a community that shares their search and can show grounds for hope in its present experience of fellowship and social concern. If we are honest, therefore, we do not sweep them through the preparation for and reception of confirmation in a peer group that generates a kind of herd pressure and gets them through with little conviction of their own. This would show little respect for the young people but it would also show little respect for the serious nature of the sacrament and for the serious nature of the community that continues to build itself out of the accretion of such newcomers.

Because of the nature of sin and the nature of salvation from sin, the Church is essentially, not accidentally, concerned with every one of these problems that concretely constitute the disorientation and alienation of the persons living in our time and culture. To bring into the Church should mean to bring into a community that lives in a reconciled manner, that is to say a community that constantly serves the needy, embraces the excluded, makes peace, is concerned to reshape the economy so that it serves the interests of all, respects the dignity of all, confronts every kind of suffering with courage and compassion and lives in mutual acceptance and support in a spirit of great hope and joy. This is what the newcomer should find. This is apologetic, the demonstration of the reasonable grounds of credibility which can reasonably be expected.

In the context of such a community Christian initiation has its full meaning and efficacy as an entrance into salvation. It is the ideal. Because we live in the confusion of a sinful history in which the wheat of redemption is much intertwined with the tares of original sin, we seldom find a community that really combines all of these qualities in a significant number of its members, relationships and structures. Yet even if there is a serious striving after such attitudes and lifestyle in a small core group in a parish, there is a strong testimony to the ongoing process of redemption. Moreover, the whole manner of redemption is grace, gift, surprise, breakthrough in impossible situations. To be joined to the Church means always more than becoming a member of the local congregation of believers. It means becoming a member of the great tradition that reaches into our times from Jesus and his earliest followers. It means becoming heir to all that the great tradition has to offer, and a member of the universal community of followers of Jesus spanning centuries, continents and disparate cultures.

Excerpt from *A Rite of Passage*
By Aidan Kavanaugh

I have always rather liked the gruff robustness of the first rubric for baptism found in a late fourth-century church order which directs that the bishop enter the vestibule of the baptistery and say to the catechumens without commentary or apology only four words: "Take off your clothes. . . ."

> **Catechumens**
>
> Catechumens are unbaptized persons who have presented themselves for entrance into the Church, have been accepted into the Order of Catechumens, and have begun the process of Christian initiation. In our current day, the Rite of Christian Initiation of Adults (RCIA), based on the initiation practices of the early Church, is the normative process by which unbaptized adults are accepted into the Church and is a process of formal study, reflection, service, and prayer.

The catechumens are standing around a pool let into the middle of the floor, into which gushes water pouring noisily from the mouth of a stone lion crouching atop a pillar at poolside. The bishop stands beside this, his presbyters on each side: a deacon has entered the pool, and the other assistants are trying to maintain a modicum of decorum among the catechumens who forget their nakedness as they crowd close to see. The room is warm, humid, and it glows. . . .

The bishop rumbles a massive prayer—something about the Spirit and the waters of life and death—and then pokes the water a few times with his cane. The catechumens recall Moses doing something like that to a rock from which water flowed, and they are mightily impressed. Then a young male catechumen of about ten, the son of pious parents, is led down into the pool by the deacon. The water is warm (it has been heated in a furnace), and the oil on his body spreads out on the surface in iridescent swirls. The deacon positions the child near the cascade from the lion's mouth. The bishop leans over on his cane, and in a voice that sounds like something out of the Apocalypse, says: "Euphemius! Do you believe in God the Father, who created all of heaven and earth?" After a nudge from the deacon beside him, the boy murmurs that he does. And just in time, for the deacon, who has been doing this for fifty years and is the boy's grandfather, wraps him in his arms, lifts him backwards into the rushing water and forces him under the surface. The old deacon smiles through his beard at the wide brown eyes that look up at him in shock and fear from beneath the water (the boy has purposely not been told what to expect). Then he raises him up coughing and sputtering. The bishop waits until he can speak again, and leaning over a second time, tapping the boy on the shoulder with his cane, says: "Euphemius! Do you believe in Jesus Christ, God's only Son, who was conceived of the Virgin Mary, suffered under Pontius Pilate, and was crucified, died, and was buried? Who rose on the third day and ascended into heaven, from whence he will come again to judge the living and the dead?" This time he replies like a shot, "I do," and then holds his nose. . . . "Euphemius! Do you believe in the Holy Spirit, the master and giver of life, who proceeds from the Father, who is to be honored and glorified equally with the Father and the Son, who spoke by the Prophets? And in one holy, catholic, and apostolic Church which is the communion of God's holy ones? And in the life that is coming?" "I do."

When he comes up the third time, his vast grandfather gathers him in his arms and carries him up the steps leading out of the pool. There another deacon roughly dries Euphemius with a warm towel, and a senior presbyter, who is almost ninety and is regarded by all as a "confessor" because he was imprisoned for the faith as a young man, tremulously pours perfumed oil from a glass pitcher over the boy's damp head until it soaks his hair and runs down over his upper body. The fragrance of this enormously expensive oil fills the room as the old man mutters: "God's servant, Euphemius, is anointed in the name of the Father, Son, and Holy Spirit." Euphemius is then wrapped in a new linen tunic; the fragrant chrism seeps into it, and he is given a burning terracotta oil lamp and told to go stand by the door and keep quiet. Meanwhile, the other baptisms have continued.

When all have been done in this same manner (an old deaconess, a widow, replaced Euphemius's grandfather when it came the women's time), the clergy strike up the Easter hymn, "Christ is risen from the dead, he has crushed death by his death and bestowed life on those who lay in the tomb." To this constantly repeated melody interspersed with the Psalm verse, "Let God arise and smite his enemies," the whole baptismal party—tired, damp, thrilled, and oily—walk out into the blaze of Easter morning and go next door to the church led by the bishop. There he bangs on the closed doors with his cane: they are flung open, the endless vigil is halted, and the baptismal party enters as all take up the hymn, "Christ is risen . . . ," which is all but drowned out by the ovations that greet Christ truly risen in his newly-born ones. As they enter, the fragrance of chrism fills the church: it is the Easter-smell, God's grace olfactorally incarnate. The pious struggle to get near the newly baptized to touch their chrismed hair and rub its fragrance on their own faces. All is chaos until the baptismal party manages to reach the towering ambo that stands in the middle of the pewless hall. The bishop ascends its lower front steps, turns to face the white-clad neophytes grouped at the bottom with their burning lamps and the boisterous faithful now held back by a phalanx of well-built acolytes and doorkeepers. Euphemius's mother has fainted and been carried outside for some air.

The bishop opens his arms to the neophytes and once again all burst into "Christ is risen," *Christos aneste*. . . . He then affirms and seals their baptism after prayer, for all the Faithful to see, with an authoritative gesture of paternity—laying his hand on each head, signing each oily forehead once again in the form of a cross, while booming out: "The servant of God is sealed with the Holy Spirit." To which all reply in a thunderous "Amen," and for the first time the former catechumens receive and give the kiss of peace. Everyone is in tears.

While this continues, bread and wine are laid out on the holy table; the bishop then prays at great length over them after things quiet down, and the neophytes lead all to communion with Euphemius out in front. While his grandfather holds his lamp, Euphemius dines on the precious Body whose true and undoubted member he has become; drinks the precious Blood of him in whom he himself has now died; and just this once drinks from two other special cups—one containing baptismal water, the other containing milk and honey mixed as a gustatory icon of the promised land into which he and his colleagues have finally entered out of the desert through Jordan's waters. Then his mother (now recovered and somewhat pale, still insisting she had only stumbled) took him home and put him, fragrantly, to bed.

Euphemius had come a long way. He had passed from death into a life he lives still.

For Reflection

1. After reading the selections, how would you describe the importance of living in community for Christians?

2. In "Christian Initiation: Gate to Salvation," Monika Hellwig describes young people who possess "certain felt needs for salvation, certain deprivations, fears and sufferings from which they know they need to be rescued, certain perceptions of what is wrong and unjust in the world which they know must be changed." Is this true for you? Explain.

3. As you read *A Rite of Passage*, were you able to imagine the rites of Christian initiation in the early Church? How do you think the theology described in "Christian Initiation: Gate to Salvation" and *Lumen Gentium* are symbolized in *A Rite of Passage*?

9 The Sacrament of Baptism

Introduction

In your studies of liturgy, you may have run across the phrases *ex opere operato and ex opere operantis*. These two Latin phrases are vital to understanding God's work and our work in the sacraments. Translated into English, *ex opere operato* roughly means "the work worked." For an action to be a sacrament in the Catholic Church, four things must be in place: (1) the proper materials must be used, (2) the proper words must be said, (3) the proper person must minister, and (4) the intention to act in harmony with the Church must exist. If these four things are present, the sacrament "works."

In the case of **Baptism**, an inerasable mark is placed upon a person's soul, and Christ forever claims that person. A family can present an infant to the Church for Baptism, or an adult may ask for Baptism. In both cases in the Sacrament of Baptism, a permanent mark is placed on the person's soul, and the infant or adult belongs to God. This happens because the Sacrament has been given (*ex opere operato*). What about our freedom and our choice? Why do some baptized people seem not to act in Christian ways? Baptized people have done many terrible things. If the Sacrament actually worked, how could such people do bad things?

Sacrament of Baptism The first of the Seven Sacraments and one of the three Sacraments of Christian Initiation (the others being Confirmation and the Eucharist) by which one becomes a member of the Church and a new creature in Christ.

If *ex opere operato* is one side of the coin, *ex opere operantis* is the other side. Yes, the Sacrament of Baptism places a permanent mark on a soul, but each person has a choice and freedom to

64

say yes to God's will for his or her life. If the "work" of the Sacrament brings the gift of God's presence, how will the recipient of the Sacrament respond? *Ex opere operantis* roughly means "the work of the worker." The grace of God, the gift of God's very presence, is freely given in the Sacrament of Baptism, but it does not do our work for us. Each recipient of Baptism has the responsibility to cooperate with God's activity. God does not force his will on us. We must freely choose it.

This chapter provides two readings from the Church's Tradition. At the Ecumenical Council of Florence (1438–1445), the Church defined the four points mentioned on page 64. See if you can identify the proper material and the proper words, or "form," for Baptism in this reading. It also describes how Baptism takes away both Original Sin and the sins a person commits. Picking up on the effects of Baptism, which makes us children of God and members of the Body of Christ, the Church, a short excerpt from *Lumen Gentium* describes the need for the baptized to go into the world to spread the Good News of Jesus.

Our next reading is a theological homily from Pope Benedict XVI. You can see that he is a former professor and a great teacher. He names his points and then explains them. He says: "Baptism is adoption and admission into God's family, into communion with the Most Holy Trinity, into communion with the Father, the Son and the Holy Spirit." This is his thesis statement. Watch how he develops these points.

These readings develop the wonderful and deep mystery of Baptism. However, theology is meant to bring people to a different way of living. Earlier, this chapter's introduction mentioned that an inerasable mark is placed on a person's soul at Baptism. The baptized person is marked and claimed for Christ. The chapter's final reading is a story of how being claimed for Christ and being brought into God's family is made real for one family.

Excerpt from the Ecumenical Council of Florence

By the Council of Florence

> ### Indelibly on the Soul a Character
>
> Saint Augustine gave the Church the language of "indelible character" to describe the permanence of Christ's claim on a baptized person. It is forever and cannot be removed by anything the person does or does not do.

There are seven sacraments of the new Law, namely baptism, confirmation, eucharist, penance, extreme unction, orders and matrimony, which differ greatly from the sacraments of the **old Law**. The latter were not causes of grace, but only prefigured the grace to be given through the passion of Christ; whereas the former, ours, both contain grace and bestow it on those who worthily receive them. The first five of these are directed to the spiritual perfection of each person in himself, the last two to the regulation and increase of the whole church.

For, by baptism we are reborn spiritually; by confirmation we grow in grace and are strengthened in faith. Once reborn and strengthened, we are nourished by the food of the divine eucharist. But if through sin we incur an illness of the soul, we are cured spiritually by penance. Spiritually also and bodily as suits the soul, by extreme unction. By orders the church is governed and spiritually multiplied; by matrimony it grows bodily.

All these sacraments are made up of three elements: namely, things as the matter, words as the form, and the person of the minister who confers the sacrament with the intention of doing what the church does. If any of these is lacking, the sacrament is not effected.

Three of the sacraments, namely baptism, confirmation and orders, imprint indelibly on the soul a character, that is a kind of

> **old Law** Divine Law revealed in the Old Testament, summarized in the Ten Commandments. Also called the Law of Moses. It contrasts with the New Law of the Gospels.

stamp which distinguishes it from the rest. Hence they are not repeated in the same person. The other four, however, do not imprint a character and can be repeated.

Holy baptism holds the first place among all the sacraments, for it is the gate of the spiritual life; through it we become members of Christ and of the body of the church. Since death came into the world through one person, unless we are born again of water and the spirit, we cannot, as **Truth** says, enter the kingdom of heaven. The matter of

> ❝ *For, by baptism we are reborn spiritually; by confirmation we grow in grace and are strengthened in faith. Once reborn and strengthened, we are nourished by the food of the divine eucharist.* ❞

this sacrament is true and natural water, either hot or cold. The form is: I baptize you in the name of the Father and of the Son and of the holy Spirit. But we do not deny that true baptism is conferred by the following words: May this servant of Christ be baptized in the name of the Father and of the Son and of the holy Spirit; or, This person is baptized by my hands in the name of the Father and of the Son and of the holy Spirit. Since the holy Trinity is the principal cause from which baptism has its power and the minister is the instrumental cause who exteriorly bestows the sacrament, the sacrament is conferred if the action is performed by the minister with the invocation of the holy Trinity. The minister of this sacrament is a priest, who is empowered to baptize in virtue of his office. But in case of necessity not only a priest or a deacon, but even a lay man or a woman, even a pagan and a heretic, can baptize provided he or she uses the form of the church and intends to do what the church does. The effect of this sacrament is the remission of all original and actual guilt, also of all penalty that is owed for that guilt. Hence no satisfaction for past sins is to be imposed on the baptized, but those who die before they incur any guilt go straight to the kingdom of heaven and the vision of God. . . .

With regard to children, since the danger of death is often present and the only remedy available to them

Truth Name for Jesus. In John's Gospel, Jesus says he is "the way, and the truth, and the life" (14:6).

is the sacrament of baptism by which they are snatched away from the dominion of the devil and adopted as children of God, it admonishes that sacred baptism is not to be deferred for forty or eighty days or any other period of time in accordance with the usage of some people, but it should be conferred as soon as it conveniently can; and if there is imminent danger of death, the child should be baptized straightaway without any delay, even by a lay man or a woman in the form of the church, if there is no priest. . . .

Excerpt from *Dogmatic Constitution on the Church (Lumen Gentium)*

By the Second Vatican Council

17. As the Son was sent by the Father, (Cf. Jn. 20:21) so He too sent the Apostles, saying: "Go, therefore, make disciples of all nations, baptizing them in the name of the Father and of the Son and of the Holy Spirit, teaching them to observe all things whatsoever I have commanded you. And behold I am with you all days even to the consummation of the world." (Mt. 2:18–20) The Church has received this solemn mandate of Christ to proclaim the saving truth from the apostles and must carry it out to the very ends of the earth. (Cf. Acts 1:8) Wherefore she makes the words of the Apostle her own: "Woe to me, if I do not preach the Gospel," (1 Cor. 9:16) and continues unceasingly to send heralds of the Gospel until such time as the infant churches are fully established and can them-selves continue the work of evangelizing. For the Church is compelled by the Holy Spirit to do her part that God's plan may be fully realized, whereby He has constituted Christ as the source of salvation for the whole world. By the proclamation of the Gospel she prepares her hearers to receive and profess the faith. She gives them the dispositions necessary for baptism, snatches them from the slavery of error and of idols and incor-porates them in Christ so that through charity they may grow up into full maturity in Christ. Through her work, whatever good is in the minds and hearts of men, whatever good lies latent in the religious practices and cultures of diverse peoples, is not only saved from destruction but is also

cleansed, raised up and perfected unto the glory of God, the confusion of the devil and the happiness of man. The obligation of spreading the faith is imposed on every disciple of Christ, according to his state. Although, however, all the faithful can baptize, the priest alone can complete the building up of the Body in the eucharistic sacrifice. Thus are fulfilled the words of God, spoken through His prophet: "From the rising of the sun until the going down thereof my name is great among the gentiles, and in every place a clean oblation is sacrificed and offered up in my name." (Mal. 1:11)[1]

> ❝ *Through her [the Church's] work, whatever good is in the minds and hearts of men, whatever good lies latent in the religious practices and cultures of diverse peoples, is not only saved from destruction but is also cleansed, raised up and perfected unto the glory of God, the confusion of the devil and the happiness of man.* ❞

In this way the Church both prays and labors in order that the entire world may become the People of God, the Body of the Lord and the Temple of the Holy Spirit, and that in Christ, the Head of all, all honor and glory may be rendered to the Creator and Father of the Universe.

Endnote

1. Cfr. Didache, 14: ed. Funk I, p. 32. S. Iustinus, Dial. 41: PG 6, 564. S. Irenaeus, Adv. Haer. IV 17, 5; PG 7, 1023; Harvey, 2, p. 199 s. Conc. Trid., Sess. 22, cap. 1; Denz. 939 (1742).

Excerpt from "Homily of His Holiness Benedict XVI, Feast of the Baptism of the Lord"

By Pope Benedict XVI

Dear Brothers and Sisters,

This year too, we are meeting for a real family celebration, the Baptism of 13 children in this wonderful Sistine Chapel, where with their creativity, Michelangelo and other outstanding artists achieved masterpieces that illustrate the wonders of the history of salvation.

I would like immediately to greet all of you present here: the parents, the godparents, the relatives and friends who accompany these newborn babies at such an important moment for their lives and for the Church. Every child who is born brings us God's smile and invites us to recognize that life is his gift, a gift to be welcomed with love and preserved with care, always and at every moment. . . .

At this moment we can think that Heaven has also opened here, above these children of ours who, through the Sacrament of Baptism, come into contact with Jesus. Heaven opens above us in the Sacrament. The more we live in contact with Jesus in the reality of our Baptism, the more Heaven will open above us. And from Heaven—let us return to the Gospel—that day a voice came which said to Jesus: "You are my beloved Son" (*Lk* 3:22).

In Baptism, the Heavenly Father also repeats these words for each one of these infants. He says: "You are my child." Baptism is adoption and admission into God's family, into communion with the Most Holy Trinity, into communion with the Father, the Son and the Holy Spirit. For this very reason, Baptism should be administered in the Name of the Most Holy Trinity. These words are not merely a formula; they are reality. They mark the moment when your children are reborn as children of God.

Body and Soul

As human beings, we are both body and spirit. Each human person is a single being: body and soul joined in union. The word *soul* refers to the spiritual and life-giving principle within us. Together, body and soul, spirit and matter, make a living, human body, able to praise God by its very existence. For this reason, we may not harm our bodies but honor them as God's creation and as temples of the Holy Spirit.

From being the children of human parents, they also become the children of God in the Son of the living God.

However, we must now meditate on the words in the Second Reading of this liturgy where St Paul tells us: "He saved us, not because of deeds done by us in righteousness, but in virtue of his own mercy, by the washing of regeneration and renewal in the Holy Spirit" (*Ti* 3:5).

A washing of regeneration: Baptism is not only a word, it is not only something spiritual but also implies matter. All the realities of the earth are involved. Baptism does not only concern the soul. Human spirituality invests the totality of the person, body and soul. God's action in Jesus Christ is an action of universal efficacy. Christ took flesh and this continues in the sacraments in which matter is taken on and becomes part of the divine action.

We can now ask precisely why water should be the sign of this totality. Water is the element of fertility. Without water there is no life. Thus, in all the great religions water is seen as the symbol of motherhood, of fruitfulness. For the Church Fathers, water became the symbol of the maternal womb of the Church.

Tertullian, a Church writer of the second and third centuries, said something surprising. He said: "Never is Christ without water." By these words, Tertullian meant that Christ is never without the Church. In Baptism we are adopted by the Heavenly Father, but in this family that he establishes there is also a mother, Mother Church. Man cannot have God as Father, the ancient Christian writers were already saying, unless he has the Church as mother.

We perceive in a new way that Christianity is not merely an individual, spiritual reality, a simple subjective decision that I take, but something real and concrete, we could also say something material. Adoption as children of God, of the Trinitarian God, is at the same time being accepted into the family of the Church, it is admission as brothers and sisters into the great family of Christians. And only if, as children of God, we are integrated as brothers and sisters into the reality of the Church can we say "Our Father," to our Heavenly Father. This prayer always implies the "we" of God's family.

> 66 *Adoption as children of God, of the Trinitarian God, is at the same time being accepted into the family of the Church, it is admission as brothers and sisters into the great family of Christians.* 99

Now, however, let us return to the Gospel in which John the Baptist says: "I baptize you with water; but he who is mightier than I is coming . . . he will baptize you with the Holy Spirit and with fire" (*Lk* 3:16).

We have seen water; but now the question is unavoidable: of what does the fire that St John the Baptist referred to consist? To see this reality of the fire, present in Baptism with water, we must note that John's baptism was a human gesture, an act of penance, a human impulse for God, to ask the forgiveness of sins and the chance to begin a new life. It was only a human desire, a step towards God with their own effort.

Now this is not enough. The distance would be too great. In Jesus Christ we see that God comes to meet us. In Christian Baptism, instituted by Christ, we do not only act with the desire to be cleansed through the prayer to obtain forgiveness.

In Baptism God himself acts, Jesus acts through the Holy Spirit. In Christian Baptism the fire of the Holy Spirit is present. God acts, not only us. God is present here today. He takes on your children and makes them his own.

But naturally, God does not act in a magical way. He acts only with our freedom. We cannot renounce our freedom. God challenges our freedom, invites us to cooperate with the fire of the Holy Spirit. These two things must go together. Baptism will remain throughout life a gift of God, who has set his seal on our souls. But it will then be our cooperation, the availability of our freedom to say that "yes" which makes divine action effective.

> **Seal**
>
> The Pope uses the word *seal* to mean the same thing as *indelible character, indelible mark,* and *claimed by Christ*. In the Eastern Churches, Confirmation is conferred immediately after Baptism. During the chrismation (confirmation) rite, the priest anoints each bodily sense (eyes, ears, hands, feet) with the myron (chrism), and to each anointing the assembly responds: *Seal!*

These children of yours, whom we will now baptize, are not yet able to collaborate, to manifest their faith. For this reason, your presence, dear fathers and mothers, and yours, dear godfathers and godmothers, acquires a special value and significance. Always watch over your little ones, so that they may learn to know God as they grow up, love him with all their strength and serve him faithfully. May you be their first educators in faith, offering together with your teaching also the examples of a coherent Christian life. Teach them to pray and to feel as living members of the concrete family of God, of the Ecclesial Community.

The attentive study of the *Catechism of the Catholic Church* or of the *Compendium* of this *Catechism* can offer you important help. It contains the essential elements of our faith and can be a particularly useful and immediate means, for you yourselves, to grow in the knowledge of the Catholic faith and to transmit it integrally and faithfully to your children. Above all, do not forget that it is your witness, it is your example, that has the greatest effect on the human and spiritual maturation of your children's freedom. Even caught up in the sometimes frenetic daily activities, do not neglect to foster prayer, personally and in the family, which is the secret of Christian perseverance.

Let us entrust these children and their families to the Virgin Mother of Jesus, Our Saviour, presented in today's liturgy as the beloved Son of God: may Mary watch over them and accompany them always, so that they can fully carry out the project of salvation which God has for each one. Amen.

Excerpt from *Pastoral Foundations of the Sacraments: A Catholic Perspective*
By Gregory L. Klein and Robert A. Wolfe

Sarah took the baby in her arms and sat down in the rocker with a great deal of pleasure. It was a wonderful rocker. It creaked and rolled with her, and the sounds comforted her like an old friend. The baby looked up at her, and with a lovely yawn, gently fell off to sleep.

Sarah rocked the baby and hummed a lullaby tune that sprang from the love in her heart. She knew the tune but was not sure anyone else knew it. It was a lullaby that had been born of sitting in this same rocker, rocking children of her youth. It was a private song of a mother to a child that no one else really needed to know.

Sarah simply enjoyed the moment. It had been such a full and wonderful day. She, who would normally be in the kitchen organizing things, or out visiting, was quite content to leave all of that business to others, and claimed these precious moments with this baby all to herself. Back and forth she rocked, matching the rhythms of the innocent child's breathing. What could be better than this? With her humming and rocking, Sarah made herself and the baby so comfortable that the noise of the departing guests could be pleasantly ignored.

Sarah remembered the day that her husband had brought this old rocker home. It had been such a big purchase for him. Things were tight in those days, and most luxuries had to be avoided. But this rocker was a gift of his love for her. He bought it on a payment plan he really couldn't afford, but took the risk because he wanted her to know that he would be a part of the difficult days of her pregnancy and the early days of raising their children. Sometimes it's just good to keep some old things around. She had comforted, fed and nourished five newborn babies in this chair, but rarely had a moment of rocking been so satisfying for her.

Sarah shifted her weight and rearranged the baby close to herself, she noticed a peculiar smell on the crown of the baby's head. "What is this?" she thought as she drew closer for inspection. There was a strange odor, not like any shampoo or lotion for babies that she knew of. This was like a spice from the orient. What could it be? Yes. It was the oil of baptism.

Sarah began to remember the ceremony. There were many babies. Sarah was sure that no baby was more wanted or loved than the baby she held in her arms. This granddaughter was her first. She had been waiting a very long time for this child. Her son and his wife discovered shortly after marriage that they would not be able to have children of their own. They had only envisioned their marriage as one with children. On the day the doctor had told them of their situation, they began the long process of adoption.

The adoption process had been filled with a great deal of emotion. Sarah's son had been most cooperative, even to the point of denying his deep disappointment of their situation. There had been many promises made to the couple over the years about when and what type of child might be available to them. There was one occasion when the adoption agency had promised the young couple that a child would be born and ready for them in one week. There was so much excitement and preparations made. Sarah brought her wonderful well-used rocker as a gift to the expectant parents. The birth mother changed her mind one day after the birth. The grief in the house was profound. The only way Sarah could comfort her son was to insist that they keep the rocker for another day. Another day and another child had come.

There had been so much cautious expectation over this chosen child that Sarah listened to the words of baptism more carefully than before. She heard something she had not remembered, although she was sure it had been said over her own five children. The priest said at the very beginning over the child, "I claim you for Christ our Savior by the sign of the cross." She knew how much her son and daughter-in-law wanted this child, how they claimed it for their own. Now there were new words said. "I claim you for Christ our Savior."

The baby began to stir, and Sarah called to the mother: "It's time for you to take your Julie." As she got up out of the old rocker and passed the baby to her mother, Sarah resolved that she would do everything a grandmother could do to raise a child that was chosen, loved and claimed for Christ.

For Reflection

1. The reading from *Lumen Gentium* describes the call you received at Baptism to bring the Good News to the world. On a scale of one to ten, how committed are you to bringing the Good News to the world? Explain.

2. In the homily by Pope Benedict XVI, the Pope mentions prayer as an important part of fostering the relationship with God that comes through Baptism. Why do you think he specifically mentions prayer? How could you incorporate more prayer in your daily routine?

3. Being claimed by Christ our Savior is a theme that is present throughout this chapter. After reading this chapter, how would you describe being claimed by Christ as you understand it?

10 The Sacrament of Confirmation

Introduction

The work of the Second Vatican Council can be simplified to two words: *recover* and *update*. The Council recognized that the Church has a rich and beautiful tradition. It also recognized there was confusion about things that were essential to being a disciple of Jesus and about practices that had run their course and were no longer needed. The Church wanted first to recover those things that are central to being Catholic. The second step was to update the freshly understood truths the Church had recovered. These truths needed to be expressed in a way that was relevant to a new time and to new places. The **Sacrament of Confirmation** received this attention.

As you have seen in the readings in chapter 8, "Sacraments of Christian Initiation," and chapter 9, "The Sacrament of Baptism," there is a unity between Baptism and Confirmation. This is what the Church wanted to recover: that Confirmation completes Baptism. The Eastern Catholic Churches and Orthodox Christians speak of "grafting" and "vivification." In John's Gospel Jesus describes himself as the vine and those who follow him as the branches. When people are baptized, they are like branches grafted onto a vine. To become fully part of the vine, sap must flow into

Sacrament of Confirmation With Baptism and the Eucharist, one of the three Sacraments of Christian Initiation. Through an outpouring of special Gifts of the Holy Spirit, Confirmation completes the grace of Baptism by confirming or "sealing" the baptized person's union with Christ and by equipping that person for active participation in the life of the Church.

the branch to bond it fully. When it has bonded with the vine, the branch grows leaves and is able to bear fruit—it becomes vivified, or enlivened. Vivification completes the grafting as Confirmation completes Baptism.

In our first reading, the "Apostolic Constitution on the Sacrament of Confirmation," Pope Paul VI affirms the Second Vatican Council's work of recovery. He wrote this constitution several years after the Second Vatican Council, when the Church updated the rite, or the ceremony, in which the Sacrament of Confirmation is conferred. The Pope wanted the Rite of Confirmation to clearly reveal that the Holy Spirit is the Gift that is given. The Holy Spirit enlivens those confirmed, draws them more fully into the Church, and gives them power to be witnesses.

In our second reading, Pope Benedict XVI wanted to convey this last point to the young pilgrims at the 2008 World Youth Day in Sydney, Australia. You will notice that Pope Benedict uses the word *vivifying*. His homily, given at the vigil the night before he conferred Confirmation on young people from around the world, explains what *vivification* means. A life lived in the Holy Spirit is a life of communion in God, the God who is love. This love is to transform every part of our lives and our world. The Pope is clear that the Holy Spirit brings this power of love and transformation.

The chapter's third reading, an excerpt from the article "What Difference Does Confirmation Make?" by Joseph Martos, reflects on the experience of the Sacrament itself. Although the Holy Spirit does come in power at Confirmation, that power isn't always immediately felt. Some people experience something that is indeed transformative. Others detect nothing profound happening. Yet the fruits of this Sacrament are still evident for those who say yes to the gift of the Holy Spirit.

Excerpt from "Apostolic Constitution on the Sacrament of Confirmation"

By Pope Paul VI

The sharing in the divine nature received through the grace of Christ bears a certain likeness to the origin, development, and nourishing of natural life. The faithful are born anew by baptism, strengthened by the sacrament of confirmation, and finally are sustained by the food of eternal life in the eucharist. By means of these sacraments of Christian initiation, they thus receive in increasing measure the treasures of divine life and advance toward the perfection of charity. It has rightly been written: "The body is washed, that the soul may be cleansed; the body is signed, that the soul too many be fortified; the body is overshadowed by the laying on of hands, that the soul may be enlightened by the Spirit; the body is fed on the body and blood of Christ, that the soul may be richly nourished by God."[1]

Conscious of its pastoral charge, the Second Vatican Ecumenical Council devoted special attention to these sacraments of initiation. It prescribed that the rites should be revised in a way that would make them more suited to the understanding of the faithful. Since the Rite of Baptism for Children, revised at the mandate of the Council and published at our command, is already in use, it is now fitting to publish a rite of confirmation, in order to show the unity of Christian initiation in its true light.

In fact, careful attention and application have been devoted in these last years to the task of revising the manner of celebrating this sacrament. The aim of this work has been that "the intimate connection of this sacrament with the whole of Christian initiation may stand out more clearly."[2] But the link between confirmation and the other sacraments of initiation is more easily perceived not simply from the fact that their rites have been more closely conjoined; the rite and words by which confirmation is conferred also make this link clear. As a result the rite and words of this sacrament "express more clearly the holy things they signify and the Christian people, as far as possible, are able to understand them with ease and take part in them fully, actively, and as befits a community."[3]

For that purpose, it has been our wish also to include in this revision what concerns the very essence of the rite of confirmation, through which the faithful receive the Holy Spirit as a Gift.

The New Testament shows how the Holy Spirit was with Christ to bring the Messiah's mission to fulfillment. On receiving the baptism of John, Jesus saw the Spirit descending on him (see Mk 1:10) and remaining with him (see Jn 1:32). He was led by the Spirit to undertake his public ministry as the Messiah, relying on the Spirit's presence and assistance. Teaching the people of Nazareth, he showed by what he said that the words of Isaiah, "The Spirit of the Lord is upon me," referred to himself (see Lk 4:17–21).

He later promised his disciples that the Holy Spirit would help them also to bear fearless witness to their faith even before persecutors (see Lk 12:12). The day before he suffered, he assured his apostles that he would send the Spirit of truth from his Father (see Jn 15:26) to stay with them "for ever" (Jn 14:16) and help them to be his witnesses (see Jn 15:26). Finally, after his resurrection, Christ promised the coming descent of the Holy Spirit: "You will receive power when the Holy Spirit comes upon you; then you are to be my witnesses" (Acts 1:8; see Lk 24:49).

On the feast of Pentecost, the Holy Spirit did indeed come down in an extraordinary way on the apostles as they were gathered together with Mary the mother of Jesus and the group of disciples. They were so "filled with" the Holy Spirit (Acts 2:4) that by divine inspiration they began to proclaim "the mighty works of God." Peter regarded the Spirit who had thus come down upon the apostles as the gift of the Messianic age (see Acts 2:17–18). Then those who believed the apostles' preaching were baptized and they too received "the gift of the Holy Spirit" (Acts 2:38). From that time on the apostles, in fulfillment of Christ's wish, imparted to the newly baptized by the laying on of hands the gift of the Spirit that completes the grace of baptism. This is why the Letter to the Hebrews listed among the first elements of Christian instruction the teaching about baptisms and the laying on of hands (Heb 6:2). This laying on of hands is rightly recognized by reason of Catholic tradition as the beginning of the sacrament of confirmation, which in a certain way perpetuates the grace of Pentecost in the Church.

This makes clear the specific importance of confirmation for sacramental initiation, by which the faithful "as members of the living Christ are incorporated into him and configured to him through baptism and through confirmation and the eucharist."[4] In baptism, the newly baptized receive forgiveness of sins, adoption as children of God, and the character of Christ by which they are made members of the Church and for the first time become sharers in the priesthood of their Savior (see 1 Pt 2:5, 9). Through the sacrament of confirmation those who have been born anew in baptism receive the inexpressible Gift, the Holy Spirit himself, by whom "they are endowed . . . with special strength."[5] Moreover, having been signed with the character of this sacrament, they are "more closely bound to the Church"[6] and "they are more strictly obliged to spread and defend the faith, both by word and by deed, as true witnesses of Christ."[7] Finally, confirmation is so closely linked with the holy eucharist[8] that the faithful, after being signed by baptism and confirmation, are incorporated fully into the Body of Christ by participation in the eucharist.[9]

> 66 *Through the sacrament of confirmation those who have been born anew in baptism receive the inexpressible Gift, the Holy Spirit himself, by whom 'they are endowed . . . with special strength.'* 99

From ancient times the conferring of the gift of the Holy Spirit has been carried out in the Church through various rites. These rites have undergone many changes in the East and the West, but always keeping as their meaning the conferring of the Holy Spirit. . . .

From what we have recalled, it is clear that in the administration of confirmation in the East and the West, though in different ways, the most important place was occupied by the anointing, which in a certain way represents the apostolic laying on of hands. Since this anointing with chrism is an apt sign of the spiritual anointing of the Holy Spirit who is given to the faithful, we wish to confirm its existence and importance.

As regards the words pronounced in confirmation, we have examined with the consideration it deserves the dignity of the respected formulary used in the Latin Church, but we judge preferable the very ancient formulary belonging to the Byzantine Rite. This expresses the Gift of the Holy Spirit himself and calls to mind the outpouring of the Spirit on the day of Pentecost (see Acts 2:1–4, 38). We therefore adopt this formulary, rendering it almost word for word.

Therefore, in order that the revision of the rite of confirmation may, as is fitting, include even the essence of the sacramental rite, by our supreme apostolic authority we decree and lay down that in the Latin Church the following are to be observed for the future.

The sacrament of confirmation is conferred through the anointing with chrism on the forehead, which is done by the laying on of the hand, and through the words: be sealed with the gift of the holy spirit. . . .

Endnotes

1. Tertullian, *De resurrection mortuorum* 8, 3: CCL 2, 931.
2. *Sacrosanctum Concilium* art. 71.
3. *Sacrosanctum Concilium* art. 21.
4. *Ad Gentes* no. 36.
5. *Lumen Gentium* no. 11.
6. *Lumen Gentium* no. 11.
7. *Ibid.* See also *Ad Gentes* no. 11.
8. See *Presbyterorum Ordinis* no. 5.
9. See *ibid.*

Excerpt from "Address of His Holiness Benedict XVI on the Occasion of the 23rd World Youth Day, 2008"

By Pope Benedict XVI

Dear Young People,

Once again this evening we have heard Christ's great promise—"you will receive power when the Holy Spirit has come upon you." And we have heard his summons—"be my witnesses throughout the world"—(*Acts* 1:8). These were the very last words which Jesus spoke before his Ascension into heaven. How the Apostles felt upon hearing them, we can only imagine. But we do know that their deep love for Jesus, and their trust in his word, prompted them to gather and to wait; to wait not aimlessly, but together, united in prayer, with the women and Mary in the Upper

Room (cf. *Acts* 1:14). Tonight, we do the same. Gathered before our much-travelled Cross and the icon of Mary, and under the magnificent constellation of the Southern Cross, we pray. Tonight, I am praying for you and for young people throughout the world. Be inspired by the example of your Patrons! Accept into your hearts and minds the sevenfold gift of the Holy Spirit! Recognize and believe in the power of the Spirit in your lives! . . .

Tonight we focus our attention on *how* to become witnesses. We need to understand the person of the Holy Spirit and his vivifying presence in our lives. This is not easy to comprehend. Indeed the variety of images found in scripture referring to the Spirit—wind, fire, breath—indicate our struggle to articulate an understanding of him. Yet we do know that it is the Holy Spirit who, though silent and unseen, gives direction and definition to our witness to Jesus Christ. . . .

Friends, when reciting the Creed we state: "We believe in the Holy Spirit, the Lord, the giver of life." The "Creator Spirit" is the power of God giving life to all creation and the source of new and abundant life in Christ. The Spirit sustains the Church in union with the Lord and in fidelity to the apostolic Tradition. He inspired the Sacred Scriptures and he guides God's People into the fullness of truth (cf. *Jn* 16:13)[.] In all these ways the Spirit is the "giver of life," leading us into the very heart of God. So, the more we allow the Spirit to direct us, the more perfect will be our configuration to Christ and the deeper our immersion in the life of the Triune God.

This sharing in God's nature (cf. 2 *Pet* 1:4) occurs in the unfolding of the everyday moments of our lives where he is always present (cf. *Bar* 3:38). There are times, however, when we might be tempted to seek a certain fulfilment apart from God. Jesus himself asked the Twelve: "do you also wish to go away?" Such drifting away perhaps offers the illusion of freedom. But where does it lead? To whom would we go? For in our hearts we know that it is the Lord who has "the words of eternal life" (*Jn* 6:67–68). To turn away from him is only a futile attempt to escape from ourselves (cf. Saint Augustine, *Confessions* VIII, 7). God is with us in the reality of life, not the fantasy! It is embrace, not escape, that we seek! So the Holy Spirit gently but surely steers us back to what is real, what is lasting, what is true. It is the Spirit who leads us back into the communion of the Blessed Trinity!

The Holy Spirit has been in some ways the neglected person of the Blessed Trinity. A clear understanding of the Spirit almost seems beyond our reach. Yet, when I was a small boy, my parents, like yours, taught me the Sign of the Cross. So, I soon came to realize that there is one God in three Persons, and that the Trinity is the centre of our Christian faith and life. While I grew up to have some understanding of God the Father and the Son—the names already conveyed much—my understanding of the third person of the Trinity remained incomplete. So, as a young priest teaching theology, I decided to study the outstanding witnesses to the Spirit in the Church's history. It was on this journey that I found myself reading, among others, the great Saint Augustine. . . .

Dear young people, we have seen that it is the Holy Spirit who brings about the wonderful communion of believers in Jesus Christ. True to his nature as giver and gift alike, he is even now working through you. Inspired by the insights of Saint Augustine: let *unifying love* be your measure; *abiding love* your challenge; *self-giving love* your mission!

Tomorrow, that same gift of the Spirit will be solemnly conferred upon our confirmation candidates. I shall pray: "give them the spirit of wisdom and understanding, the spirit of right judgement and courage, the spirit of knowledge and reverence . . . and fill them with the spirit of wonder and awe." These gifts of the Spirit—each of which, as Saint Francis de Sales reminds us, is a way to participate in the one love of God—are neither prizes nor rewards. They are freely given (cf. *1 Cor* 12:11). And they require only one response on the part of the receiver: I accept! Here we sense something of the deep mystery of being Christian. What constitutes our faith is not primarily what we do but what we receive. After all, many generous people who are not Christian may well achieve far more than we do. Friends, do you accept being drawn into God's Trinitarian life? Do you accept being drawn into his communion of love?

The Spirit's gifts working within us give direction and definition to our witness. Directed to unity, the gifts of the Spirit bind us more closely to the whole Body of Christ (cf. *Lumen Gentium,* 11), equipping us better to build up the Church in order to serve the world (cf. *Eph* 4:13). They call us to active and joyful participation in the life of the Church: in parishes and ecclesial movements, in religious education classes, in university chaplaincies

> 66 *Just as the Church travels the same journey with all humanity, so too you are called to exercise the Spirit's gifts amidst the ups and downs of your daily life. Let your faith mature through your studies, work, sport, music and art. Let it be sustained by prayer and nurtured by the sacraments, and thus be a source of inspiration and help to those around you.* 99

and other catholic organizations. Yes, the Church must grow in unity, must be strengthened in holiness, must be rejuvenated, must be constantly renewed (cf. *Lumen Gentium,* 4). But according to whose standard? The Holy Spirit's! Turn to him, dear young people, and you will find the true meaning of renewal.

Tonight, gathered under the beauty of the night sky, our hearts and minds are filled with gratitude to God for the great gift of our Trinitarian faith. We recall our parents and grandparents who walked alongside us when we, as children, were taking our first steps in our pilgrim journey of faith. Now many years later, you have gathered as young adults with the **Successor of Peter.** I am filled with deep joy to be with you. Let us invoke the Holy Spirit: he is the artisan of God's works (cf. *Catechism of the Catholic Church,* 741). Let his gifts shape you! Just as the Church travels the same

Successor of Peter Another title for the Pope. Saint Peter is recognized as the first Bishop of Rome. The Pope, as the Bishop of Rome, has succeeded Peter in that ministry.

journey with all humanity, so too you are called to exercise the Spirit's gifts amidst the ups and downs of your daily life. Let your faith mature through your studies, work, sport, music and art. Let it be sustained by prayer and nurtured by the sacraments, and thus be a source of inspiration and help to those around you. In the end, life is not about accumulation. It is much more than success. To be truly alive is to be transformed from within, open to the energy of God's love. In accepting the power of the Holy Spirit you too can transform your families, communities and nations. Set free the gifts! Let wisdom, courage, awe and reverence be the marks of greatness!

Excerpts from "What Difference Does Confirmation Make?"

By Joseph Martos

It's been a long time, but I can remember it well. The 40 of us were lined up in the schoolyard on a cold day, our red "graduation" robes blowing in the wind. We were only in the fifth grade, but we were allowed to wear the robes for Confirmation—red being the color the Church uses to represent the Holy Spirit. We felt very grown-up, and very proud.

An hour later, as far as I could tell, it was over. We had been anointed (blessed with oil) on the forehead and slapped lightly on the cheek. In those days, that "slap" told us that we had to be "soldiers of Christ," ready to suffer for our faith. We had sung "Come, Holy Ghost," and the bishop had prayed over us and put his hand on our head. I felt like I had been ordained or surely something as important and official as that.

I look back on that day of years ago and ask myself, what difference did it make? It was a nice ceremony—almost like a parade or a welcome-home celebration. And of course there was the party afterwards and the Confirmation presents. But really, I didn't understand how much of a welcome it was and to what!

My wife tells me that, for her, the sacrament did make a big difference right away. I was glad to hear that on her Confirmation day she felt the love and power of God in a special way. She began to pray more, and

attended Mass on weekdays. She made a constant effort to be more helpful at home, to be more polite to her parents, and to be less quarrelsome
with her sisters—and she felt the grace within her to succeed. . . .

Different experiences of Confirmation are matched by different re-
sponses to the sacrament and its graces. In talking about my wife, I said
that she not only felt something different at her Confirmation, but she
also behaved differently afterwards. On the other hand, I don't remember behaving any differently right after I was confirmed, although I can
honestly say that if I weren't a confirmed Christian I might have lived
my life very differently over the years. And I'm sure that there are people
whose Confirmation has never, ever made any difference whatsoever in
their life. But there again, most people fall somewhere between the two
extremes. . . .

. . . Confirmation can make a real difference in the lives of young
people. It can give you a chance to think about your baptism and about
what it means to be a Christian. When you were baptized as an infant,
you didn't know what was happening. Now, when you are older, you
have a chance to reaffirm your membership in the Church and to say
your own "I do" to your baptismal promises.

So Confirmation can indeed make a difference in your life. It can
have the effect of a special spiritual awakening, as it had for my wife. Or
it can have the effect of being a special reminder of your commitment to
Christ and to the Church, as it was for me. A lot depends on you, and
on the circumstances surrounding your own Confirmation.

For Reflection

1. The readings emphasize the power of the Holy Spirit at Confirmation. The power is to enable someone to be a witness for Jesus. Do you think it is easy or difficult for today's teens to be a witness for Jesus? Explain.

2. Pope Benedict XVI said: "Let your faith mature through your studies, work, sport, music and art." Which of these do you most identify with? How do you think these things can be witnesses for Jesus through the Holy Spirit?

3. Recall the third reading, by Joseph Martos. If you have been confirmed, which experience was most like yours: Martos's or his wife's? If you have not been confirmed, which experience do you relate to more? Explain.

11 The Sacrament of the Eucharist

Introduction

The **Sacrament of the Eucharist** is known by many names. This is in itself an acknowledgment of its richness. The Eucharist is also called the Breaking of Bread, the memorial of the Lord's Passion and Resurrection, the Holy Sacrifice, Holy Mass, and Holy Communion. One name in particular seems to sum up all the others and to indicate the unique place the Eucharist has in our Christian lives: the Eucharist is "the Sacrament of sacraments" (*Catechism of the Catholic Church [CCC]*, 1211). Why? Because this is the Sacrament toward which all the others lead, for in the Eucharist we encounter the Real Presence of Christ under the appearances of bread and wine. In the Eucharist Christ is physically present with us through the mystery of **Transubstantiation**.

At the Council of Nicaea, in AD 325, the Church used the term *consubstantial* to describe Jesus. This word meant that Jesus is God in the exact same way that the Father is God. Their substance is the same. The word *Transubstantiation* builds upon this important word, *substance*. Of the wide variety of topics we could choose

> **Sacrament of the Eucharist** Also called the Mass or Lord's Supper, and based on a word for "thanksgiving," it is the central Christian liturgical celebration, established by Jesus at the Last Supper. In the Eucharist the sacrificial death and Resurrection of Jesus are both remembered and renewed. The term sometimes refers specifically to the consecrated bread and wine that have become the Body and Blood of Christ.
>
> **Transubstantiation** In the Sacrament of the Eucharist, this is the name given to the action of changing the bread and wine into the Body and Blood of Jesus Christ.

in our discussion of the Eucharist, we will focus in this chapter on the Eucharist as the Body and Blood of Christ. In the Eucharist we encounter the Real Presence of Jesus, who calls us to communion with him and with one another.

Our first reading is from the Council of Trent (1545–1563). That council officially defined the Eucharist as a change in substance. In simple terms, that which was bread is no longer bread. That which was wine is no longer wine. The Eucharistic elements of bread and wine become the real Body and real Blood of Jesus. It is the Body and Blood of Christ not just during the liturgy; it is also forever changed.

Throughout the Christian centuries, two questions have caused deep reflection on the teaching of Transubstantiation. How does it become the Body and Blood of Christ? Why does it become the Body and Blood of Christ? Chapter 3 in this book had a reading from Edward Schillebeeckx's book *Christ the Sacrament of the Encounter with God.* In that book Schillebeeckx makes the point that all the Sacraments share an *epiclesis,* a calling down of the Holy Spirit. In this chapter's second reading, Saint John Damascene (676–749) devotes some thought to this. He recalls the many miracles God has worked throughout the ages. Of particular note, he reminds the reader that Mary became pregnant with Jesus through the Holy Spirit. This moment could be thought of as a kind of *epiclesis.* That miracle continues in the Eucharist. The Holy Spirit is invoked and is asked to transform the bread and wine into Jesus' Body and Jesus' Blood. This answers *how* they are transformed. *Why* are the bread and wine transformed? The Council of Trent, Saint John Damascene, and Jean Vanier all declare that the purpose of Transubstantiation is to take away sin and bring us to communion.

Jean Vanier, cofounder of the L'Arche Christian communities, brings us this chapter's third reading. The L'Arche communities have been established to bring disabled people together with those without disabilities. They are together to help one another become the people God intends them to be. Vanier reflects on his experience of living with those who are vulnerable in light of Jesus' washing of the disciples' feet at the Last Supper. He brings communion from a concept to a reality.

All the readings in this chapter emphasize that the bread and wine are changed into the Body and Blood of Christ so that, in receiving Jesus Christ, we may be changed. As we receive Jesus, he becomes part of us, and we also become part of him. The Eucharist is given so that we may be brought into communion with Jesus and all of his Body, the Church.

Excerpt from *Canons and Decrees of the Council of Trent*
By the Council of Trent

Chapter I: The Real Presence of Our Lord Jesus Christ in the Most Holy Sacrament of the Eucharist

First of all, the holy council teaches and openly and plainly professes that after the consecration of bread and wine, our Lord Jesus Christ, true God and true man, is truly, really and substantially contained in the august sacrament of the Holy Eucharist under the appearance of those sensible things. For there is no repugnance in this that our Savior sits always at the right hand of the Father in heaven according to the natural mode of existing, and yet is in many other places sacramentally present to us in His own substance by a manner of existence which, though we can scarcely express in words, yet with our understanding illumined by faith, we can conceive and ought most firmly to believe is possible to God. [Matt. 19:26; Luke 18:27] For thus all our forefathers, as many as were in the true Church of Christ and who treated of this most holy sacrament, have most openly professed that our Redeemer instituted this

> **No Repugnance in This**
>
> In the early Church and during the Middle Ages, some people believed it was unfitting, or repugnant, for God to take the form of bread and wine.

wonderful sacrament at the last supper, when, after blessing the bread and wine, He testified in clear and definite words that He gives them His own body and His own blood. Since these words, recorded by the holy Evangelists [Matt. 26:26–28; Mark 14:22–24; Luke 22:19 f.] and afterwards repeated by St. Paul, [See 1 Cor. 11:24 f.] embody that proper and clearest meaning in which they were understood by the Fathers, it is a most contemptible action on the part of some contentious and wicked men to twist them into fictitious and imaginary tropes by which the truth of the flesh and blood of Christ is denied, contrary to the universal sense of the Church, which, as the pillar and ground of truth, [See 1 Tim. 3:15] recognizing with a mind ever grateful and unforgetting this most excellent favor of Christ, has detested as satanical these untruths devised by impious men.

> **Forefathers . . . Have Most Openly Professed**
>
> Discovering and maintaining the constant, unbroken teaching of Christ, the Council wants to show that the belief in Transubstantiation is the constant teaching of the Church.

Chapter II: The Reason for the Institution of This Most Holy Sacrament

Therefore, our Savior, when about to depart from this world to the Father, instituted this sacrament, in which He poured forth, as it were, the riches of His divine love towards men, making a remembrance of his wonderful works, [Ps. 110:4] and commanded us in the participation of it to reverence His memory and to show forth his death until he comes [Luke 22:19; 1 Cor. 11:24–26] to judge the world. But He wished that this sacrament should be received as the spiritual food of souls, [Matt. 26:26 f.] whereby they may be nourished and strengthened, living by the life of Him who said: He that eateth me, the same also shall live by me, [John 6:58] and as an antidote whereby we may be freed from daily faults and be preserved from mortal sins.

He wished it furthermore to be a pledge of our future glory and everlasting happiness, and thus be a symbol of that one body of which He is the head [See 1 Cor. 11:3; Eph. 5:23] and to which He wished us to be united as members by the closest bond of faith, hope and charity, that we might all speak the same thing and there might be no schisms among us [See 1 Cor. 1:10]. . . .

> **Whole Substance**
>
> The elements of bread and wine have fully and completely become the Body and Blood of Christ, although they appear not to have changed.

Chapter IV: Transubstantiation

But since Christ our Redeemer declared that to be truly His own body which He offered under the form of bread, [Luke 22:19; John 6:48 ff.; 1 Cor. 11:24] it has, therefore, always been a firm belief in the Church of God, and this holy council now declares it anew, that by the consecration of the bread and wine a change is brought about of the whole substance of the bread into the substance of the body of Christ our Lord, and of the whole substance of the wine into the substance of His blood. This change the holy Catholic Church properly and appropriately calls transubstantiation.

> 66 *By the consecration of the bread and wine a change is brought about of the whole substance of the bread into the substance of the body of Christ our Lord, and of the whole substance of the wine into the substance of His blood. This change the holy Catholic Church properly and appropriately calls transubstantiation.* 99

Chapter V: The Worship and Veneration to Be Shown to This Most Holy Sacrament

There is, therefore, no room for doubt that all the faithful of Christ may, in accordance with a custom always received in the Catholic Church, give to this most holy sacrament in veneration the worship of *latria*, which is due to the true God. Neither is it to be less adored for the reason that it was instituted by Christ the Lord in order to be received. [Matt. 26:26] For we believe that in it the same God is present of whom the eternal Father, when introducing Him into the world, says: And let all the angels of God adore him; [Heb. 1:6] whom the Magi, falling down, adored; [Matt. 2:11] who, finally, as the Scriptures testify, was adored by the Apostles in Galilee [Ibid., 28:17—Luke 24:52]. . . .

Chapter VII:
The Preparation to Be Employed That One May Receive the Sacred Eucharist Worthily

If it is unbecoming for anyone to approach any of the sacred functions except in a spirit of piety, assuredly, the more the holiness and divinity of this heavenly sacrament are understood by a Christian, the more diligently ought he to give heed lest he receive it without great reverence and holiness, especially when we read those terrifying words of the Apostle: "He that eateth and drinketh unworthily, eateth and drinketh judgment to himself, not discerning the body of the Lord." [See 1 Cor. 11:29] Wherefore, he who would communicate, must recall to mind his precept: "Let a man prove himself." [Ibid., 11:28] Now, ecclesiastical usage declares that such an examination is necessary in order that no one conscious to himself of

Latria

There are three forms of honor and devotion: *dulia, hyperdulia,* and *latria. Dulia* is the honor given to the saints and angels. *Hyperdulia* is the reverence given to Mary, the Mother of God. *Latria* is given to God alone. The Blessed Sacrament is the Real Presence of Jesus, fully God and fully human. Because Jesus is fully God, *latria* is the kind of honor given to the Blessed Sacrament.

Adore Him

The council makes the case for the practice of Eucharistic adoration. Because it is actually the Body and Blood of Christ, it is right that the Eucharist be worshipped and adored outside Mass.

mortal sin, however contrite he may feel, ought to receive the Sacred Eucharist without previous sacramental confession. This the holy council has decreed to be invariably observed by all Christians, even by those priests on whom it

may be incumbent by their office to celebrate, provided the opportunity of a confessor is not wanting to them. But if in an urgent necessity a priest should celebrate without previous confession, let him confess as soon as possible.

Mortal sin Sin is mortal, or deadly, when it separates the Christian from God and the rest of the Body of Christ. The council says that one who is separated from the Body of Christ (the Church) must be reunited with the Body of Christ before receiving the Eucharist.

Excerpt from "Concerning the Holy and Immaculate Mysteries of the Lord," from *De Fide Orthodoxa,* Book 4, Chapter 13

By Saint John Damascene

In the upper chamber, then, of holy and illustrious **Sion**, after He had eaten the ancient Passover with His disciples and had fulfilled the ancient covenant, He washed His disciples' feet [St. John xiii] in token of the holy baptism. Then having broken bread He gave it to them saying, Take, eat, this is My body broken for you for the remission of sins. [St. Matt. xxvi.26; Liturg. S. Jacobi.] Likewise also He took the cup of wine and water and gave it to them saying, Drink ye all of it: for this is My blood, the blood of the New Testament which is shed for you for the remission of sins. This do ye in remembrance of Me. For as often as ye eat this bread and drink this cup, ye do shew the death of the Son of man and confess His resurrection until He come. [St. Matt. xxvi.27, 28; St. Mark xiv.22–24; St. Luke xxii.19, 20; 1 Cor. xi.24–26]

If then the Word of God is quick and energising, [Heb. iv.12] and the Lord did all that He willed; [Ps. cxxxv.6] if He said, Let there be light and there was light, let there be a firmament and there was a firmament; [Gen. i.3 and 6] if the heavens were established by the Word of the Lord and all the host of them by the breath of His mouth; [Ps. xxxiii.6] if the heaven and the earth, water and fire and air and the whole glory of these, and, in sooth, this most noble creature, man, were perfected by the Word of the Lord; if God the Word of His own will became man and the pure and undefiled blood of the holy and ever-virginal One made His flesh without the aid of seed, can He not then make the bread His body and the wine and water His blood? He said in the beginning, Let the earth

Sion *Sion*, or *Zion*, is a term used to describe Jerusalem as a heavenly city. It is a reference to the city, sometimes called New Jerusalem, that God will establish when he fully establishes his Reign. This renewed society in which God dwells is also a symbol of the Church, the "holy city," the assembly of the People of God called together from "the ends of the earth."

bring forth grass, [Gen. i. 11] and even until this present day, when the rain comes it brings forth its proper fruits, urged on and strengthened by the divine command. God said, This is My body, and This is My blood, and this do ye in remembrance of Me. And so it is at His omnipotent command until He come: for it was in this sense that He said until He come: and the overshadowing power of the Holy Spirit becomes through the invocation the rain to this new tillage. For just as God made all that He made by the energy of the Holy Spirit, so also now the energy of the Spirit performs those things that are supernatural and which it is not possible to comprehend unless by faith alone. How shall this be, said the holy Virgin, seeing I know not a man? And the archangel Gabriel answered her: The Holy Spirit shall come upon thee, and the power of the Highest shall overshadow thee. [St. Luke i.34, 35] And now you ask, how the bread became Christ's body and the wine and water Christ's blood. And I say unto thee, "The Holy Spirit is present and does those things which surpass reason and thought."

Further, bread and wine are employed: for God knoweth man's infirmity: for in general man turns away discontentedly from what is not well-worn by custom: and so with His usual indulgence He performs His supernatural works through familiar objects: and just as, in the case of baptism, since it is man's custom to wash himself with water and anoint himself with oil, He connected the grace of the Spirit with the oil and the water and made it the water of regeneration, in like manner since it is man's custom to eat and to drink water and wine, He connected His divinity with these and made them His body and blood in order that we may rise to what is supernatural through what is familiar and natural. . . .

> 66 *The bread and the wine are not merely figures [representations] of the body and blood of Christ (God forbid!) but the deified body of the Lord itself: for the Lord has said, 'This is My body,' not, this is a figure of My body: and 'My blood,' not, a figure of My blood.* 99

The bread and the wine are not merely figures of the body and blood of Christ (God forbid!) but the deified body of the Lord itself: for the

Lord has said, "This is My body," not, this is a figure of My body: and "My blood," not, a figure of My blood. And on a previous occasion He had said to the Jews, Except ye eat the flesh of the Son of Man and drink His blood, ye have no life in you. For My flesh is meat indeed and My blood is drink indeed. . . . [St. John vi.51–55]

The body and blood of Christ are making for the support of our soul and body, without being consumed or suffering corruption, not making for the **draught** (God forbid!) but for our being and preservation, a protection against all kinds of injury, a purging from all uncleanness: should one receive base gold, they purify it by the critical burning lest in the future we be condemned with this world. They purify from diseases and all kinds of calamities; according to the words of the divine Apostle, For if we would judge ourselves, we should not be judged. But when we are judged, we are chastened of the Lord, that we should not be condemned with the world. This too is what he says, So that he that partaketh of the body and blood of Christ unworthily, eateth and drinketh damnation to himself. Being purified by this, we are united to the body of Christ and to His Spirit and become the body of Christ. . . .

Participation is spoken of; for through it we partake of the divinity of Jesus. Communion, too, is spoken of, and it is an actual communion, because through it we have communion with Christ and share in His flesh and His divinity: yea, we have communion and are united with one another through it. For since we partake of one bread, we all become one body of Christ and one blood, and members one of another, being of one body with Christ.

draught An obsolete word meaning "privy" or "sewer." Pronounced "draft."

Excerpt from "Homily of Jean Vanier at Lambeth Vigil (Second Service)"

By Jean Vanier

You know that in the Gospels of Luke and Matthew and Mark, at this last important meal, Jesus institutes the Eucharist. Here in the Gospel of John, it doesn't talk at all about the institution of the Eucharist. He talks only about the washing of each other's feet. It is a little sign that these two realities—the institution of the Eucharist and the washing of each other's feet—should not be separated. We are called to eat the Body of Christ so that we can wash each other's feet, and wash the feet of the poor and the lame, the broken and the blind.

I would like to go a little bit deeper and ask why does Jesus wash our feet? And why does he ask us to wash each other's feet? What is the signification behind it? . . .

Our hands are, in some mysterious way, a source of revelation of communion. Jesus, as he knelt down in front of the feet of his disciples, knows that tomorrow he will be dead. But he wants to have with each disciple a moment. Not just to say goodbye. Up until now he has just talked with the group. When you talk with a whole group you don't have that individual contact with each person. Jesus wants that contact with each one of these people. He wants to touch them—to touch their feet; to touch their bodies; to touch them with tenderness and love. Maybe to each one he says a word; maybe looks each one in the eye. There is a moment of communion.

So there is communion through the Body of Christ, where Jesus says "do this in memory of me." But there is also this communion as he kneels at their feet. And later he will say "I have done this as an example for you. And what I have done to you, you must do one to another." So this is a gesture of communion, of tenderness.

Jesus touched their bodies—a realization that each one is the Temple of God. "Do you not know that your body is the temple of the Spirit. The Spirit of God is living in you." I believe that Jesus must have touched these bodies with an immense respect and love and tenderness. He was revealing to them, in a special way, his love for them. But he also revealed to them that each one of them is beautiful, is chosen, and is loved. To continue this mission, which is his mission, to announce the good news to the poor, freedom to captives, sight to the blind, liberty to the oppressed, and to announce a year of grace and forgiveness. . . .

. . . Jesus washes the feet in a sense of cleansing. But also, Jesus is there on his knees as a servant, as a slave—to be there for us. There is something inconceivable that the Lord and master, in this flimsy tunic washing our feet, says to us "I want to serve you; I want to empower you. Because you will receive the Holy Spirit. And you must continue what I have done. You must be filled with the Spirit of God, so that you can go out to the ends of the earth, to bring that love to all people of all cultures."

. . . We want to be in communion—one with another. We love each other. We may have divergences in vision, divergences in theological questions. This is normal. We come from cultures and backgrounds that are very different. Each one of us, we have our character traits. We have the wound in us. We have our fragility and our need to prove that "I am better than you." So Jesus is saying something about communion—how to be with each other with words that [are] not flowing from our wound-edness, our darkness, and our need for power and superiority, but from a desire for oneness. And oneness is not exclusion of difference. Oneness is not fusion. Saint Paul says we are all different. It is the recognition of difference. But that doesn't mean to say that we crush difference.

So we are called to be in communion, to forgive each other, to serve each other, and to discover that together we are all called to walk the downward path. We are all called to be small. "The camel cannot go through the eye of the needle." But we who carry authority and power, in some way we are called to be like little children. And we are called to serve each other in rectitude and in truth as Jesus. And as we become small, then maybe we can go through the eye of the needle.

And so this evening, that is what we are going to do. We do so in a witness of our desire to follow the humble Jesus, the broken Jesus, and the weeping Jesus—the Jesus who became little and humbled himself even more. In some way we want to follow Jesus on that downward path. This is the path which, as we go down, then with him we rise again to be a sign of resurrection in our world.

For Reflection

1. As taught by the Council of Trent, at the Eucharistic liturgy, the bread and wine are changed (transubstantiated) into the Body and Blood of Christ. Use the commentary of Saint John Damascene to explain how this happens.

2. Saint John Damascene recalls the words of Jesus as he says that the Body and Blood have been given for the forgiveness of sins. Explain the connection between the forgiveness of sin and Communion.

3. The homily from Jean Vanier says that Jesus' act of washing the feet of his disciples at the Last Supper is a lesson that the Eucharist is to lead to communion through service. In real and practical ways, how can you serve your family, your school, and your Church to bring about greater communion?

4. Christians have long been asking the question, "Why did Jesus give the Eucharist to the Church?" How would you answer this question for today?

Part 3
The Sacraments of Healing

12 Healing of Soul and Body

Introduction

On the first day of class, an old and wise theology professor walked into the classroom. He looked at the blank stares of his graduate students and started by shouting: "What is the purpose of the Church?!" The blank stares became looks of terror. No one answered. "Can none of you graduate students who are devoting three years of your lives to studying theology tell me why there is a Church?!" he shouted again. He let the question hang in the air. He remained silent and let the question deeply sink into the students' minds. After several moments, he leaned onto his podium and whispered, "Reconciliation. Reconciliation is the mission of the Church."

This chapter's first reading, from "Decree *Ad Gentes* on the Mission Activity of the Church," is the declaration from the Second Vatican Council that describes the Church's missionary activity. That mission is to reconcile all things to God the Father through Jesus Christ. It is a mission to continue the works and mission of Jesus in the world. In proclaiming the Good News of Jesus, the Church tells the world "what has not been taken up by Christ is not made whole" (*Mission Activity of the Church*, 3). This might seem like an odd phrase, but the Good News lies in the fact that everything, the entire human condition, has been "taken up by Christ." He took upon himself human suffering, physical and psychological. Even though he did not sin, he took up the sin of humanity. For this reason, the **Sacraments of Healing** (the Sacrament

Sacraments of Healing The two Sacraments instituted by Christ for the healing of soul and body: the Sacrament of Penance and Reconciliation and the Sacrament of Anointing of the Sick.

of Anointing of the Sick and the Sacrament of Penance and Reconciliation) are not "add-on" Sacraments. Rather, they are vital parts of Christ's ministry. Because reconciliation and healing are Christ's ministry, they are the Church's as well.

The second reading, by German Martinez, introduces a term that has recently gained in popularity: *integral salvation*. The Catholic view of the human person holds no true distinction between the body and soul: "The unity of soul and body is so profound that one has to consider the soul to be the 'form' of the body:[1] i.e., it is because of its spiritual soul that the body made of matter becomes a living, human body; spirit and matter, in man, are not two natures united, but rather their union forms a single nature" (*CCC*, 365). Because of this unity, salvation and restoration are a spiritual-bodily event. Jesus' miracles of restoration and healing take on a new meaning. They are acts of kindness, indeed, but they are more than that. They reveal life in the Kingdom of God. This Kingdom is a reign of wholeness in body, mind, and soul.

Finally, in our third reading, we find a moving story about an integral healing. Two alcoholic men struggle together and seek God's healing, reconciliation, and restoration.

Excerpt from "Decree *Ad Gentes* on the Mission Activity of the Church"
By the Second Vatican Council

Preface

1. Divinely sent to the nations of the world to be unto them "a universal sacrament of salvation," the Church, driven by the inner necessity of her own **catholicity**, and obeying the mandate of her Founder

catholicity Along with One, Holy, and Apostolic, *Catholic* is one of the four marks of the Church. *Catholic* means "universal." The Church is catholic in two senses. She is catholic because Christ is present in her and has given her the fullness of the means of salvation and also because she reaches throughout the world to people of all times, cultures, races, and geographies.

(cf. Mark 16:16), strives ever to proclaim the Gospel to all men. The Apostles themselves, on whom the Church was founded, following in the footsteps of Christ, "preached the word of truth and begot churches." It is the duty of their successors to make this task endure "so that the word of God may run and be glorified (2 Thess. 3:1) and the kingdom of God be proclaimed and established throughout the world." . . .

Chapter 1: Principles of Doctrine

3. This universal design of God for the salvation of the human race is carried out not only, as it were, secretly in the soul of a man, or by the attempts (even religious ones by which in diverse ways it seeks after God) if perchance it may contact Him or find Him, though He be not far from anyone of us (cf. Acts 17:27). For these attempts need to be enlightened and healed; even though, through the kindly workings of Divine Providence, they may sometimes serve as leading strings toward God, or as a preparation for the Gospel. Now God, in order to establish peace or the communion of sinful human beings with Himself, as well as to fashion them into a fraternal community, did ordain to intervene in human history in a way both new and finally sending His Son, clothed in our flesh, in order that through Him He might snatch men from the power of darkness and Satan (cf. Col. 1:13; Acts 10:38) and reconcile the world to Himself in Him. Him, then, by whom He made the world, (cf. Hebrews 1:2; John 1:3 and 10; 1 Cor. 8:6; Col. 1:16) He appointed heir of all things, that in Him He might restore all (cf. Eph. 1:10).

For Jesus Christ was sent into the world as a real mediator between God and men. Since He is God, all divine fullness dwells bodily in Him (Gal. 2:9). According to His human nature, on the other hand, He is the new Adam, made head of a renewed humanity, and full of grace and of truth (John 1:14). Therefore the Son of God walked the ways of a true Incarnation that He might make men sharers in the nature of God: made poor for our sakes, though He had been rich, in order that His poverty might enrich us (2 Cor. 8:9). The Son of Man came not that He might be served, but that He might be a servant, and give His life as a ransom for the many—that is, for all (cf. Mark 10:45). The Fathers of the Church proclaim without hesitation that what has not been taken up by Christ is not made whole. Now, what He took up was our entire human nature such as it is found among us poor wretches, save only sin (cf. Heb. 4:15; 9:28). For Christ said concerning Himself, He whom the Father sanctified and sent into the world (cf. John 10:36): the Spirit of the Lord is upon me, because He anointed me; to bring good news to the poor He sent me, to heal the broken-hearted, to proclaim to the captives release, and sight to the blind" (Luke 4:18). And again: "The Son of Man has come to seek and to save what was lost" (Luke 19:10). . . .

8. Missionary activity is closely bound up even with human nature itself and its aspirations. For by manifesting Christ the Church reveals to men the real truth about their condition and their whole calling, since Christ is the source and model of that redeemed humanity, imbued with brotherly love, sincerity and a peaceful spirit, to which they all aspire. Christ and the Church, which bears witness to Him by preaching the Gospel, transcend every peculiarity of race or nation and therefore cannot be considered foreign anywhere or to anybody. Christ Himself is the way and the truth, which the preaching of the Gospel opens to all in proclaiming in the hearing of all these words of Christ: "Repent, and believe the Gospel" (Mark 1:15). Now, since he who does not believe is already judged (cf. John 3:18), the words of Christ are at one and the same time words of judgment and of grace, of death and of life. For it is only by putting to death what is old that we are able to approach the newness of life. This is true first of all about persons, but it holds also for the various goods of this world which bear the mark both of man's sin and of God's blessing: "For all have sinned and have need of the glory of God" (Rom. 3:23). No one is freed from sin by himself and by his own power, no one is raised above himself, no one is completely rid of his sickness or his solitude or his servitude. On the contrary, all stand in need of Christ, their model, their mentor, their liberator, their Savior, their source of life. The Gospel has truly been a leaven of liberty and progress in human history, even in the temporal sphere, and always proves itself a leaven of brotherhood, of unity

and of peace. Not without cause is Christ hailed by the faithful as "the expected of the nations, and their Savior." (O Antiphon for Dec. 23)

9. And so the time for missionary activity extends between the first coming of the Lord and the second, in which latter the Church will be gathered from the four winds like a harvest into the kingdom of God. (Cf. Matt. 24:31, *Didache*, 10, 5, Funk I, p. 32.) For the Gospel must be preached to all nations before the Lord shall come (cf. Mark 13:10).

Missionary activity is nothing else and nothing less than an epiphany, or a manifesting of God's decree, and its fulfillment in the world and in world history, in the course of which God, by means of mission, manifestly works out the history of salvation. By the preaching of the word and by the celebration of the sacraments, the center and summit of which is the most holy Eucharist, He brings about the presence of Christ, the author of salvation. But whatever truth and grace are to be found among the nations, as a sort of secret presence of God, He frees from all taint of evil and restores to Christ its maker, who overthrows the devil's domain and wards off the manifold malice of vice. And so, whatever good is found to be sown in the hearts and minds of men, or in the rites and cultures peculiar to various peoples, not only is not lost, but is healed, uplifted, and perfected for the glory of God, the shame of the demon, and the bliss of men. . . .

Excerpt from "The Healing Ministry of Christ," from *Signs of Freedom: Theology of the Christian Sacraments*

By German Martinez

Many New Testament texts, especially the synoptic gospels, portray Jesus as a miracle worker, a compassionate physician, and a prophetic liberator. Miraculous healings (approximately twenty-five) play a prominent role in Jesus' ministry and reveal his attitude toward the sick. As John Meier states, "Nothing is more certain about Jesus than that he was viewed by his contemporaries as an exorcist and healer."[1] The healing power of his actions, such as the miracle "signs" in the Gospel of John, is directed not only toward accomplishing inner renewal through faith and trust but also toward communicating with the body, thereby touching the whole person. Moreover, Jesus' non-judgmental gentleness and unconditional compassion inspired trust and hope, which gave meaning to human sickness and suffering. Finally, as a prophetic liberator "moved with compassion," Jesus showed signs of deliverance coming from God to the people in the midst of their affliction. He proclaimed the dignity of the person by rejecting both oppressive religious laws and the culture's judgment, thus overcoming human selfishness (cf. Luke 13:10–17).

This prophetic passion for the destiny of the person makes the ministry of Jesus a living gospel of compassion, evident in the narratives of his prophetic actions. These narratives represent the faith of the early Christian communities proclaiming definitive and integral salvation. Through Christ, God designs to break the power of evil and to re-create the human condition. In fact, "Jesus' miracles are not simply kind deeds done to individuals; they were concrete ways of proclaiming and effecting God's triumph over the powers of evil in the final hour. The miracles were signs and partial realizations of what was about to come fully in the kingdom."[2]

In fact, the prophets had seen sickness in all its manifestations as an expression of the power of darkness and the slavery of the evil that would be overcome by the messianic promise (cf. Isa 35:5–6; 61:1–3; Jer 33:6). The relevant background regarding sickness, suffering, and sin needs to be clarified. Three major meanings of the experience of suffering can be emphasized in the prophetic context: (a) it is a consequence of the reality of *sin* and *punishment* for it; (b) it is a *purifying* and *learning* experience; (c) it has a *redemptive* and *healing* value.

First, suffering as a visible expression of the mystery of evil is contrary to God's will, his purpose in creation, and his covenant of fidelity. Thus, sickness and suffering were often considered the result of sin and infidelity to God's covenant. Second, in reflecting on the reality of evil as a result of sin, the just person who trusts in the Lord learns from suffering in a process of personal purification (books of Job and Tobit). Finally, within the prophetic perspective of solidarity among the chosen people of the covenant, suffering served the redemptive plan of God's salvation. . . .

Jesus rejects a fatalistic idea about the onset of sickness as personal and collective retribution for sin: "Neither this man nor his parents sinned" (John 9:1–3; cf. Jer 31:29–30). Nevertheless, God's favor calls for personal responsibility (cf. John 5:14). Thus, Jesus' prophetic teaching invited everyone to be a healing reconciler, to show compassion (Matt 5:7), especially toward the sick. To visit the sick is to visit Christ (Matt 25:36).

For Matthew, Jesus' miraculous cures realize the prophetic fulfillment: "He took our infirmities and bore our diseases" (Matt 8:17; cf. Isa 53:4). Then Matthew sums up the realization of this messianic promise in the unsurpassable healing words and wonder-working actions of Jesus:

> **Jesus' prophetic teaching invited everyone to be a healing reconciler, to show compassion (Matt 5:7), especially toward the sick. To visit the sick is to visit Christ (Matt 25:36).**

"Go and tell John what you hear and see: the blind receive their sight, the lame walk, the lepers are cleansed, the deaf hear, the dead are raised, and the poor have good news brought to them. And blessed is anyone who takes no offence at me" (Matt 11:4–6).

These external signs of healing reveal God's offer of holiness, which calls the human condition to wholeness. In the biblical mind-set, not only is the person thought of as an integrated unity of body and spirit, but holiness and God's favor are also included in bodily wholeness and integrity. This manifold perspective of inward and outward wholeness is apparent in many healing stories: the physically ill, such as the downcast leper who Jesus touched (Mark 1:40–45), are restored not only to God's friendship, but also to the fellowship of God's community; the brokenness of evil is overcome and the sick are cured (Mark 6:13); the paralytic is freed from the immobility as well as from the burden of sin (Mark 2:1–12); and the blind man recovers both his sight and his faith (John 9:35–40). Christ's redemptive holiness of grace and salvation is seen in the victory over the bonds of all evil (Matt 10:7–8). . . .

Endnotes

1. John P. Meier, "Jesus," in the *New Jerome Biblical Commentary*, ed. Raymond E. Brown et al. (Englewood Cliffs, N.J.: Prentice-Hall, 1990) 1321.
2. Ibid.

Excerpt from "A Priest on Skid Row: A City Tale of Sin and Repentance"

By Brennan Manning

A few years ago, I lay desperately sick on a motel floor in a southern city. I learned later that within a few hours, if left unattended, I would have gone into alcoholic convulsions and might have died. At that point in time I did not know I was an alcoholic. I crawled to the telephone but was shaking and quivering so badly that I could not dial. Finally, I managed one digit and got the operator. "Please help me," I pleaded. "Call Alcoholics Anonymous." She took my name and address. Within ten minutes a man walked in the door. I had never seen him before and had no idea who he was. But he had the Breath of the Father on his face and an immense reverence for my life. He scooped me up in his arms and raced me to a detox center. There began the agony of withdrawal. Anyone who has been down both sides of the street will tell you that withdrawal from alcohol can be no less severe than withdrawal from heroin.

To avoid busting into tears, I will spare the reader the odyssey of shame and pain, unbearable guilt, remorse and humiliation. But the stranger brought me back to life. His words might sound corny to you, like tired old clichés. But they were words of life to me. This fallen-away Catholic who had not been to the eucharistic table in years told me the Father loved me, that God had not abandoned me, that the Lord would draw good from what had happened. . . . He told me right now the name of the game isn't guilt and fear and shame but survival. He told me to forget about what I had lost and focus on what I had left.

He gave me an article from an American Medical Association journal explaining alcoholism as a biopsychological sickness, that an alcoholic is a biological freak that cannot stop drinking once he takes the first drink. The stranger told me to feel no more guilt than if I were recovering from some other disease like cancer or diabetes. Above all else, he affirmed me in my emptiness and loved me in my loneliness. Again and again he told me of the Father's love; how, when his children stumble and fall, he does not scold them but scoops them up and comforts them. . . . For seven days and seven nights, he breathed life into me physically and spiritually and asked nothing in return. Later I learned that he had lost his family and fortune through drinking. In his loneliness he turns on his little TV at midnight and talks to John Wayne, hoping he will talk back. Every night before bed he spends fifteen minutes reading a meditation book, praises God for his mercy, thanks him for what he has left, prays for all alcoholics, then he goes to his window, raises the shade, and blesses the world.

Two years later I returned to the same southern city. My friend still lived there, but I had no address or telephone number. So I called A.A. In one of life's tragic ironies, I learned that he was on Skid Row. He had been twelve-stepping too often (i.e., the twelfth step of the A.A. program is bringing the message of recovery to practicing alcoholics). There is a buzz word with the A.A. community—HALT. Don't let yourself get too hungry, angry, lonely, or tired or you will be vulnerable to that first drink. My friend was too burned out from helping others and went back on the sauce.

As I drove through Skid Row, I spotted a man in a doorway who I thought was my friend. He wasn't. Just another drunk wino who was neither sober nor drunk. Just dry. He hadn't had a drink in twenty-four hours and his hands trembled violently. He reached out and asked, "Hey, man, can you gimme a dollar to get some wine?"

I knelt down before him and took his hand in mine. I looked into his eyes filled with tears. I leaned over and kissed his hands. He began to cry. He didn't want a dollar. He wanted what I wanted two years earlier lying on the motel floor—to be accepted in his brokenness, to be affirmed in his worthlessness, to be loved in his loneliness. He wanted to be relieved of what Mother Teresa of Calcutta, with her vast personal experience of human misery, says is the worst suffering of all—the feeling of not being accepted or wanted. I never located my friend.

Several days later I was celebrating the Eucharist for a group of recovering alcoholics. Midway through the homily, my friend walked through the door. My heart skipped. But he disappeared during the distribution of Communion and did not return. Two days later, I received a letter from him that read in part: "Two nights ago in my own clumsy way I prayed for the right to belong, just belong among you at the holy Mass of Jesus. You will never know what you did for me last week on Skid Row. You didn't see me; but I saw you. I was standing just a few feet away in a storefront window. When I saw you kneel down and kiss that wino's hands, you wiped away from my eyes the blank stare of the breathing dead. When I saw you really cared, my heart began to grow wings, small wings, feeble wings, but wings. I threw my bottle of . . . wine down the sewer. Your tenderness and understanding breathed life into me, and I want you to know that. You released me from the shadow world of panic, fear, and self-hatred. God, what a lonely prison I was living in. Father Brennan, if you should ever wonder who Ben Shaw is, remember I am someone you know very well, I am every man you meet and every woman you meet. . . . Am I also you?"

His letter ends, "Wherever I go, sober by the grace of God one day at a time, I will thank God for you."

For Reflection

1. Why is it important that Christ took to himself all of human nature (except sin), including suffering?

2. The ministry of reconciliation brings healing to divisions. Where do you see divisions in your world, community, or school? What do you think Jesus would say regarding each of these areas?

3. Think back over the story of the alcoholic men. Explain how Christ's redemptive grace is shown as victorious over evil and suffering.

13 The Sacrament of Penance and Reconciliation

Introduction

As the **Sacrament of Penance and Reconciliation** developed from the time of Jesus until today, it took many different forms. During the Middle Ages, in some places, it sometimes took years for people to be welcomed back into a community—and the welcoming was done in a public ceremony. In other places it was done privately and looked more like today's practice. This chapter's first reading is from the Council of Trent. The council brought uniformity of practice to the Church in many areas, including the celebration of the Sacrament of Penance and Reconciliation. In this reading look for the distinctions between mortal sin and venial sin. Look for the things the priest is to do, and also look for the things the penitent, the one confessing sin, must do.

The years after the Resurrection of Jesus saw a period of extremes: extreme missionary activity and extreme persecution of the Christian Church by the Roman Empire. As a result of missionary activity, people were converting to Christianity all over the empire. In northern Africa, in the areas of modern-day Italy and Turkey, in Egypt and the Middle East, the Gospel spread and was received. As the Church grew, however, the Roman Empire perceived the Christian Church as a threat, and harsh persecutions of Christians resulted. In the face of these persecutions, many of the baptized renounced their faith. They became known as *lapsi* (LAP-see).

Sacrament of Penance and Reconciliation One of the Seven Sacraments of the Church, the liturgical celebration of God's forgiveness of sin, through which the sinner is reconciled with both God and the Church.

Once the persecution subsided, some of the *lapsi* desired to return to the Church, and this created a problem. Their testimony had caused the discovery of hidden Christian communities, and members had been put to death. Some Christians said the *lapsi* were lost, because they had been baptized and renounced the faith. They were fully aware of their actions and had permanently removed themselves from the community. Others in the community said God was always gracious and willing to forgive, even a sin as terrible as apostasy, or renouncing the faith.

In the chapter's second reading, Saint Cyprian of Carthage weighs in on the subject. Cyprian was among those who said God is always willing to forgive. He does not go easy on the *lapsi*. He lets them and others know the seriousness of the sin the *lapsi* have committed. He lets others, besides the *lapsi*, know of the seriousness of their sins as well. He says to those who have committed other serious sin: "Do we believe that a man is lamenting with his whole heart, that he is entreating the Lord with fasting, and with weeping, and with mourning, who . . . daily frequents the bathing-places with women; who, feeding at rich banquets, and puffed out with fuller dainties, belches forth on the next day his indigestions . . . ?" Harsh words. Yet, he instructs the *lapsi* to be truly sorrowful for their sins and to know God's mercy. The Church discerned that Cyprian was right and welcomed the *lapsi* back into the community through penance and forgiveness.

All this may sound much like a formula, but God is a God of surprises. In our third reading, we will hear from someone who had a surprising encounter in the Sacrament of Penance and Reconciliation.

Excerpt from the Decrees of the Council of Trent

By the Council of Trent

"I Absolve Thee . . . "

The Council of Trent provides the words necessary for the Sacrament of Penance and Reconciliation: "God, the Father of mercies, through the death and resurrection of his Son, has reconciled the world to himself and sent the Holy Spirit among us for the forgiveness of sins; through the ministry of the Church may God give you pardon and peace, and I absolve you from your sins in the name of the Father, and of the Son, and of the Holy Spirit."

Contrition, Confession, and Satisfaction

In addition to the proper words of absolution given by the Church and spoken by the proper minister of Penance, these words describe the necessary actions of the penitent in order that the Sacrament be effective: having sorrow for doing wrong ("contrition"), making the actual confession ("confession"), and working to make things right ("satisfaction").

Chapter I: The Necessity and Institution of the Sacrament of Penance

If in all those regenerated such gratitude were given to God that they constantly safeguarded the justice received in baptism by His bounty and grace, there would have been no need for another sacrament besides that of baptism to be instituted for the remission of sins. [Eph. 2:4] But since God, rich in mercy, knoweth our frame, [Ps. 102:14] He has a remedy of life even to those who may after baptism have delivered themselves up to the servitude of sin and the power of the devil, namely, the sacrament of penance, by which the benefit of Christ's death is applied to those who have fallen after baptism. . . .

Chapter III: The Parts and Fruits of This Sacrament

The holy council teaches furthermore, that the form of the sacrament of penance, in which its efficacy chiefly consists, are those words of the minister: I absolve thee, etc., to which are indeed laudably added certain prayers according to the custom of holy Church, which, however, do not by any means belong to the essence of the form nor are they necessary for the administration of the sacrament. But the acts of the penitent himself, namely, contrition, confession and satisfaction, constitute the matter of this sacrament, which acts, inasmuch as they are by God's institution required in the penitent for the integrity of the sacrament and for the full and complete remission of sins, are for this reason called the parts of penance. . . .

Chapter IV: Contrition

Contrition, which holds the first place among the aforesaid acts of the penitent, is a sorrow of mind and a detestation for sin committed with the purpose of not sinning in the future. This feeling of contrition was at all times necessary for obtaining the forgiveness of sins and thus indeed it prepares one who has fallen after baptism for the remission of sins, if it is united with confidence in the divine mercy and with the desire to perform the other things that are required

> *But since God, rich in mercy, knoweth our frame, He has a remedy of life even to those who may after baptism have delivered themselves up to the servitude of sin and the power of the devil, namely, the sacrament of penance.*

to receive this sacrament in the proper manner. The holy council declares therefore, that this contrition implies not only an abstention from sin and the resolution and beginning of a new life, but also a hatred of the old, according to the statement: "Cast away from you all your transgressions by which you have transgressed, and make to yourselves a new heart and a new spirit." [Ezech. 18:31]. . . .

Chapter V: Confession

From the institution of the sacrament of penance . . . , the universal Church has always understood that the complete confession of sins was also instituted by the Lord and is by

mortal sin An action so contrary to the will of God that it results in a complete separation from God and his grace. As a consequence of that separation, the person is condemned to eternal death. For a sin to be a mortal sin, three conditions must be met: the act must involve grave matter, the person must have full knowledge of the evil of the act, and the person must give his or her full consent in committing the act.

divine law necessary for all who have fallen after baptism; [Luke 5:14; 17:14; 1 John 1:9] because our Lord Jesus Christ, when about to ascend from earth to heaven, left behind Him priests, His own vicars, [Matt. 16:19, John 20:23] as rulers and judges, to whom all the **mortal sins** into which the faithful of Christ may have fallen should be brought in order that they may, in virtue of the power of the keys, pronounce the sentence of remission or retention of sins. For it is evident that priests could not have exercised this judgment without a knowledge of the matter, nor could they have observed justice in imposing penalties, had the faithful declared their sins in general only and not specifically and one by one.

From which it is clear that all mortal sins of which they have knowledge after a diligent self-examination, must be enumerated by the penitents in confession, even though they are most secret and have been committed only against the two last precepts of the **Decalogue**; [Deut. 5:21] which sins sometimes injure the soul more grievously and are more dangerous than those that are committed openly. **Venial sins**, on the other hand, by which we are not excluded from the grace of God and into which we fall more frequently, though they may be rightly and profitably and without any presumption declared in confession, as the practice of pious people evinces, may, nevertheless, be omitted without guilt and can be expiated by many other remedies. But since all mortal sins, even those of thought, make men "children of wrath" [Eph. 2:3] and enemies of God, it is necessary to seek pardon of all of them from God by an open and humble confession. While therefore the faithful of Christ strive to confess all sins that come to their memory, they no doubt lay all of them before the divine mercy for forgiveness; while those who do otherwise and knowingly conceal certain ones, lay nothing before the divine goodness to be

forgiven through the priest; for if one sick be ashamed to make known his wound to the physician, the latter does not remedy what he does not know. . . .

Chapter VI: The Minister of This Sacrament and Absolution

With regard to the minister of this sacrament, the holy council declares false and absolutely foreign to the truth of the Gospel all doctrines which perniciously extend the ministry of the keys to all other men besides bishops and priests, in the belief that those words of the Lord: "Whatsoever you shall bind upon earth, shall be bound also in heaven, and whatsoever you shall loose upon earth, shall be loosed also in heaven;" [Matt. 16:19; 18:18] and, "Whose sins you shall forgive, they are forgiven them, and whose sins you shall retain, they are retained," [John 20:23] were, contrary to the institution of this sacrament, addressed indifferently and indiscriminately to all the faithful of Christ in such manner that everyone has the power of forgiving sins, public ones by way of rebuke, if the one rebuked complies, and secret ones by way of a voluntary confession made to anyone. It [the council] teaches furthermore that even priests who are in mortal sin exercise, through the power of the Holy Ghost conferred in ordination, as ministers of Christ the office of forgiving sins, and that the opinion of those is erroneous who maintain that bad priests do not possess this power. . . .

Chapter VIII: The Necessity and Fruit of Satisfaction

Finally, in regard to satisfaction, which, of all the parts of penance, just as it is that which has at all times been recommended to the Christian people by our Fathers, so it is the one which chiefly in our age is under the high-sounding pretext of piety assailed by those who "have an appearance of piety, but have denied the power thereof," [See 2 Tim. 3:5] the holy council declares that it is absolutely false and contrary to the word of God, that the guilt is never remitted by the Lord without the entire punishment being remitted also. For clear and outstanding examples are found in the sacred writings, [Gen. 3:16 ff.; Num. 12:14 f.; 10:11 f.; 2 Kings 12:13 f., etc.] by

> **satisfaction** An amendment for sin. In the Sacrament of Penance and Reconciliation, the priest assigns penitents a penance to help them make amends for their sins. Particular acts of penance may include spiritual disciplines such as prayers or fasting. In particular cases exact satisfaction for sin is also required. If someone steals five dollars from another and confesses that theft, confession is not enough. The thief must also repay, or make satisfaction for, the money.

which, besides divine tradition, this error is refuted in the plainest manner. Indeed the nature of divine justice seems to demand that those who through ignorance have sinned before baptism be received into grace in one manner, and in another those who, after having been liberated from the servitude of sin and of the devil, and after having received the gift of the Holy Ghost, have not feared knowingly to violate the temple of God [See 1 Cor. 3:17] and to grieve the Holy Spirit. [Eph. 4:30] And it is in keeping with divine clemency that sins be not thus pardoned us without any **satisfaction**, lest seizing the occasion and considering sins as trivial and offering insult and affront to the Holy Spirit, [Heb. 10:29] we should fall into graver ones, "treasuring up to ourselves wrath against the day of wrath." [Rom. 2:5; James 5:3] For without doubt, these satisfactions greatly restrain from sin, check as it were with a bit, and make penitents more cautious and vigilant in the future; they also remove remnants of sin, and by acts of the opposite virtues destroy habits acquired by evil living.

Excerpt from *On the Lapsed*
By Saint Cyprian of Carthage

I entreat you, beloved brethren, that each one should confess his own sin, while he who has sinned is still in this world, while his confession may be received, while the satisfaction and remission made by the priests are pleasing to the Lord. Let us turn to the Lord with our whole heart, and, expressing our repentance for our sin with true grief, let us entreat God's mercy. Let our soul lie low before Him. Let our mourning atone to Him. Let all our hope lean upon Him. He Himself tells us in what manner we ought to ask. "Turn ye," He says, "to me with all your heart, and at the same time with fasting, and with weeping, and with mourning; and rend your hearts, and not your garments." [Joel 2:12] Let us return to the Lord with our whole heart. Let us appease His wrath and indignation with fast-ings, with weeping, with mourning, as He Himself admonishes us.

Do we believe that a man is lamenting with his whole heart, that he is entreating the Lord with fasting, and with weeping, and with mourning, who from the first day of his sin daily frequents the bathing-places with women; who, feeding at rich banquets, and puffed out with fuller dainties, belches forth on the next day his indigestions, and does not dispense of his meat and drink so as to aid the necessity of the poor? How does he who walks with joyous and glad step mourn for his death? And although it is written, "Ye shall not mar the figure of your beard," [Lev. 19:27] he plucks out his beard, and dresses his hair; and does he now study to please any one who displeases God? Or

> 66 *Let us turn to the Lord with our whole heart, and, expressing our repentance for our sin with true grief, let us entreat God's mercy.* 99

does she groan and lament who has time to put on the clothing of precious apparel, and not to consider the robe of Christ which she has lost; to receive valuable ornaments and richly wrought necklaces, and not to bewail the loss of divine and heavenly ornament? Although thou clothest thyself in foreign garments and silken robes, thou art naked; although thou adornest thyself to excess both in pearls, and gems, and gold, yet without the adornment of Christ thou art unsightly. And you who stain your hair, now at least cease in the midst of sorrows; and you who paint the edges of your eyes with a line drawn around them of black powder, now at least wash your eyes with tears. If you had lost any dear one of your friends by the death incident to mortality, you would groan grievously, and weep with disordered countenance, with changed dress, with neglected hair, with clouded face, with dejected appearance, you would show the signs of grief. Miserable creature, you have lost your soul; spiritually dead here, you are continuing to live to yourself, and although yourself walking about, you have begun to carry your own death with you. And do you not bitterly moan; do you not continually groan; do you not hide yourself, either for shame of your sin or for continuance of your lamentation? Behold, these are still worse wounds of sinning; behold, these are greater crimes—to have sinned, and not to make atonement—to have committed crimes, and not to bewail your crimes. . . .

But you, beloved brethren, whose fear is ready towards God, and whose mind, although it is placed in the midst of lapse, is mindful of its misery, do you in repentance and grief look into your sins; acknowledge the very grave sin of your conscience; open the eyes of your heart to the understanding of your sin, neither despairing of the Lord's mercy nor yet at once claiming His pardon. God, in proportion as with the affection of a Father He is always indulgent and good, in the same proportion is to be dreaded with the majesty of a judge. Even as we have sinned greatly, so let us greatly lament. To a deep wound let there not be wanting a long and careful treatment; let not the repentance be less than the sin. Think you that the Lord can be quickly appeased, whom with faithless words you have denied, to whom you have rather preferred your worldly estate, whose temple you have violated with a sacrilegious contact? Think you that He will easily have mercy upon you whom you have declared not to be your God? You must pray more eagerly and entreat; you must spend the day in grief; wear out nights in watchings and weepings; occupy all your time in wailful lamentations; lying stretched on the ground, you must cling close to the ashes, be surrounded with sackcloth and filth; after losing the raiment of Christ, you must be willing now to have no clothing; after the devil's meat, you must prefer fasting; be earnest in righteous works, whereby sins may be purged; frequently apply yourself to almsgiving, whereby souls are freed from death. [Matt. 25:36] What the adversary took from you, let Christ receive; nor ought your estate now either to be held or loved, by which you have been both deceived and conquered. Wealth must be avoided as an enemy; must be fled from as a robber; must be dreaded by its possessors as a sword and as poison. To this end only so much as remains should be of service, that by it the crime and the fault may be redeemed. Let good works be done without delay, and largely; let all your estate be laid out for the healing of your wound; let us lend of our wealth and our means to the Lord, who shall judge concerning us. Thus faith flourished in the time of the apostles; thus the first people of believers kept Christ's commands: they were prompt, they were liberal, they gave their all to be distributed by the apostles; and yet they were not redeeming sins of such a character as these.

Excerpt from "The Evangelistic Power of Sacraments"

By Shaun Gowney

Although I grew up in a catholic family, I became more casual in the practice of my faith in my teenage years and left the Church altogether when I was twenty. I disagreed with much of the Church's moral teaching and could not reconcile the idea of a merciful God with eternal damnation. So I became an agnostic. I retained a kind of personal spirituality, and observed, loosely, a more or less humanistic moral code of my own design. This brought me (and others) a great deal of grief in different ways but I did not attribute that to any serious shortcomings in my philosophy. Successes and failures alike were all part of the learning process on the road to wisdom. So each mistake was an opportunity to grow (I suppose I was rather "new-age" in my outlook but without the hippie beard and sandals). I stayed on that road for the next thirty-odd years.

Then, in 1999, both of my parents died. This led to a discussion about the afterlife one evening over supper with my sister Chris. Chris is very devout and she had been praying for me constantly throughout my agnostic decades. So she got really tearful when I told her I didn't know whether or not there was an afterlife. Then she asked me to promise her something. Without knowing what it was that she wanted me to do, I found myself saying "Okay, I will." "If I make the arrangements for you, will you go and see a priest?" she asked. "Okay" I said, again. I enjoyed a good argument and thought it might be fun to argue religion and morals with a priest. I did not for a minute think I would change my views though. I was pretty well set in my ways and felt no need to re-examine my reasons for leaving the Church.

So, about two weeks later, I found myself in a . . . sitting room with . . . Fr. Robert. I told him my story and outlined all my "conscientious" objections to catholic teaching and morality. He made a few short remarks and offered some brief explanations in passing, but mostly, he listened. I admitted that I had done many things which I sincerely regretted, but that some things I had done contrary to catholic teaching I did not regret because I did not think they were wrong. This led on to a discussion of the nature of sin and in particular of the need for sinful intent before anything could be called a sin. . . . We continued our talk for some two hours at the end of which Fr. Robert said, in the sort of voice one might use to invite someone for a cup of tea "Would you like to go to confession before you leave?" I was astounded. I said "How many hours have you got to spare?" This was not what I had come for. I didn't even remember the words you were supposed to use in confession. Fr. Robert smiled and told me that we could proceed using a question and answer approach. . . . I hesitated. This was not going the way I had imagined it at all. Then, inexplicably, I began to feel rather emotional (the Holy Spirit?), and without really knowing what I was doing I said "Okay—if you like, let's do it."

I got onto my knees, recited words to Fr. Robert's dictation and answered his questions truthfully. Before long, I was weeping and when we had done, I made my act of contrition in a voice that was cracked and broken. Then Fr. Robert pronounced the words of absolution, and made the sign of the cross over my head. I realised at that moment that even when I had said "Yes" to confession, I had not really thought I would be considered worthy of absolution. And so I could hardly believe that the sacrament had been granted to me, that I had been sacramentally reconciled with a God I hardly knew or believed in. Then I felt the forgiveness welling up inside me like a gigantic spiritual embrace. Some might say that it was just a very emotional thing—to be reminded of my many errors and failings. But I have since come to understand that the Holy Spirit was moving me at a very deep level. That was the turning point in my life.

I said my penance of three Hail Marys on the tube going home (Only three! after forty years!), and I received the Eucharist at mass the following Sunday. Since then, little by little, my faith has grown anew, only not as it had been before when I was just a schoolboy. Then it was a matter of habit, and guilt, and a fear of damnation. Now it is a source of great joy and strength. Not that I am perfect yet—not by a long way. But the change God has made in me is so great that I am daily in awe of it. I was a lump of dead wood which He grafted onto the healthy vine and by and by, I have come back to life and I have even sprouted some new green leaves. The fruit is yet to come.

For Reflection

1. How would you describe the difference between mortal and venial sins? What is the danger in considering venial sin to be "trivial"? Explain.

2. Why are contrition, confession, and satisfaction important parts of the Sacrament of Penance and Reconciliation?

3. If you lived in the time of the *lapsi,* would you have wanted to allow them back into the Church community? Explain.

4. In your own relationships, how willing are you to forgive others when you have been wronged? Do you seek out others and forgive them, or do you wait for them to come to you and apologize?

14 The Sacrament of Anointing of the Sick

Introduction

The public ministry of Jesus comprised healing and teaching. After the Resurrection, healing miracles occurred through the Apostles as well. "Peter said, 'I have neither silver nor gold, but what I do have I give you: in the name of Jesus Christ the Nazorean, [rise and] walk'" (Acts of the Apostles 3:6). The accounts from the Bible and the writings of the early Church clearly show that God is near those who are sick and suffering. Instituted by Christ, the Sacrament of Anointing of the Sick continues and makes visible God's closeness and care.

It seems that any legitimate religion must offer an answer to the question of why people suffer. It has been said that Christians should not seek an answer to the question, "Why is there evil, pain, and disease in the world?" Instead of seeking the answer to this question in philosophical pursuits, Christians should tell the story of Jesus. In Jesus, God lived among the suffering. He healed the afflicted. He also became the afflicted. Finally, he triumphed over death. This is the Christian response to the great question of pain. The **Sacrament of Anointing of the Sick** provides a ritual that invites the sick to find meaning in their suffering. They are invited to associate themselves freely with the Passion and death of Christ and eventually to rise from their death.

In 1972 the Church provided a new ritual

Sacrament of Anointing of the Sick One of the Seven Sacraments, sometimes formerly known as "the Sacrament of the dying," in which a gravely ill, aging, or dying person is anointed by the priest and is prayed over by him and attending believers. One need not be dying to receive the Sacrament.

for Anointing of the Sick. In that ritual, new words were given. The Church has an old Latin saying: *lex orandi, lex credendi*. This phrase could be translated as "the law of prayer is the law of belief." Put more simply, we believe what we pray. When a new prayer or rite is given to the Church, the time is right for a fresh, new reflection on that prayer or rite. Our chapter's first reading, from *On the Sacrament of Anointing of the Sick (Sacram Unctione Infirmorum)*, an Apostolic Constitution by Pope Paul VI, provides us with the new words and guidelines for the practice of the Sacrament. The chapter's second reading, from Regis A. Duffy, provides us with a theological reflection. In that reflection he says the Sacrament has three aspects: being united to Christ's sufferings, being communally connected, and receiving forgiveness. The third reading relates a personal experience of this Sacrament. It gives deep insight into how God makes himself present in difficult times. All the readings in this chapter explain how Jesus heals and redeems, uniting the sick to himself through the prayer of the Church community.

Excerpt from *On the Sacrament of Anointing of the Sick (Sacram Unctione Infirmorum)*

By Pope Paul VI

The Catholic Church professes and teaches that the Sacred Anointing of the Sick is one of the seven Sacraments of the New Testament, that it was instituted by Christ and that it is "alluded to in Mark (Mk. 6:13) and recommended and promulgated to the faithful by James the apostle and brother of the Lord. If any one of you is ill, he says, he should send for the elders of the church, and they must anoint him with oil in the name of the Lord and pray over him. The prayer of faith will save the sick man and the Lord will raise him up again, and if he has committed any sins, he will be forgiven (James 5:14–15)."[1]

From ancient times testimonies of the Anointing of the Sick are found in the Church's Tradition, particularly her liturgical Tradition, both in the East and in the West. Especially worthy of note in this regard are the Letter which Innocent I, our predecessor, addressed to Decentius, Bishop of Gubbio, and the venerable prayer used for blessing the Oil of the Sick: "Send forth O Lord, your Holy Spirit the Paraclete. . . ."

In the course of the centuries, in the liturgical Tradition the parts of the body of the sick person to be anointed with Holy Oil were more explicitly defined, in different ways, and there were added various formulas to accompany the anointings with prayer, which are contained in the liturgical books of various Churches. During the Middle Ages, in the Roman Church there prevailed the custom of anointing the sick on the five senses. . . .

In addition, the doctrine concerning Sacred Anointing is expounded in the documents of the Ecumenical Councils, namely the Council of Florence and in particular the Council of Trent and the Second Vatican Council.

After the Council of Florence had described the essential elements of the Anointing of the Sick, the Council of Trent declared its divine institution and explained what is given in the Epistle of Saint James concerning the Sacred Anointing, especially with regard to the reality and effects of the sacrament: "This reality is in fact the grace of the Holy Spirit, whose anointing takes away sins, if any still remain to be taken away, and the remnants of sin; it also relieves and strengthens the soul of the sick person, arousing in him a great confidence in the divine mercy, whereby

> 66 *If any one of you is ill, he [James] says, he should send for the elders of the church, and they must anoint him with oil in the name of the Lord and pray over him. The prayer of faith will save the sick man and the Lord will raise him up again, and if he has committed any sins, he will be forgiven (James 5:14–15).* 99

being thus sustained he more easily bears the trials and labors of his sickness, more easily resists the temptations of the devil 'lying in wait' (Gen. 3:15), and sometimes regains bodily health, if this is expedient for the health of the soul." The same Council also declared that in these words of the Apostle it is stated with sufficient clarity that "this anointing is to be administered to the sick, especially those who are in such a condition as to appear to have reached the end of their life, whence it is also called the sacrament of the dying." Finally, it declared that the priest is the proper minister of the sacrament.

The Second Vatican Council adds the following: "'Extreme Unction,' which may also and more fittingly be called 'Anointing of the Sick,' is not a sacrament for those only who are at the point of death. Hence, as soon as any one of the faithful begins to be in danger of death from sickness or old age, the appropriate time for him to receive this sacrament has certainly already arrived."[2] The fact that the use of this sacrament concerns the whole Church is shown by these words: "By the sacred anointing of the sick and the prayer of her priests, the whole Church commends those who are ill to the suffering and glorified Lord, asking that He may lighten their suffering and save them (cf. James 5:14–16). She exhorts them, moreover, to contribute to the welfare of the whole People of God by associating themselves freely with the passion and death of Christ (cf. Rom. 8:17; Col. 1:24; 2 Tim. 2:11–12; 1 Pt. 4:13)."[3]

All these elements had to be taken into consideration in revising the rite of Sacred Anointing, in order better to adapt to present-day conditions those elements which were subject to change.

We thought fit to modify the sacramental formula in such a way that, in view of the words of Saint James, the effects of the sacrament might be better expressed. . . .

As regards the number of anointings and the parts of the body to be anointed, it has seemed to us opportune to proceed to a simplification of the rite.

Therefore, since this revision in certain points touches upon the sacramental rite itself, by our Apostolic authority we lay down that the following is to be observed for the future in the Latin Rite:

THE SACRAMENT OF THE ANOINTING OF THE SICK IS ADMINISTERED TO THOSE WHO ARE DANGEROUSLY ILL, BY ANOINTING THEM ON THE FOREHEAD AND HANDS WITH OLIVE OIL, OR, IF OPPORTUNE, WITH ANOTHER VEGETABLE

OIL PROPERLY BLESSED, AND SAYING ONCE ONLY THE FOLLOWING WORDS: "PER ISTAM SANCTAM UNCTIONEM ET SUAM PIISSIMAM MISERICORDIAM ADIUVET TE DOMINUS GRATIA SPIRITUS SANCTI, UT A PECCATIS LIBERATUM TE SALVET ATQUE PROPITIUS ALLEVIET."

Endnotes

1. Council of Trent, Session XIV, De extr. Unct., chapter 1 (cf. ibid. canon 1): CT, VII, 1, 355–356; Denz. Schon, 1695, 1716.
2. Second Vatican Council, Const. Sacrosanctum concilium, 73:A.A.S., LVI (1964) 118–119.
3. Ibid., Const. Lumen gentium, II:A.A.S., LVII (1965) 15.

Excerpt from "Sacraments: Anointing of the Sick," from *Systematic Theology: Roman Catholic Perspectives*

By Regis A. Duffy

The . . . reform of the sacrament prompts several theological reflections. First, the anointing of the sick is rooted in the conviction that the God who creates is also the God who heals and redeems. Expressed differently, our creation in God's image and our "new creation" in Christ sketch God's redemptive plan. But within a creation

> **Within a creation not yet fully transformed, suffering and death must be experienced not as punishment, but as part of our dying and rising with Christ.**

not yet fully transformed, suffering and death must be experienced not as punishment, but as part of our dying and rising with Christ. In contrast to a purely philosophical approach to the power of evil and suffering in human existence, the gospel message proclaims God's victorious purpose as seen in the sufferings and death of Christ as validated in his resurrection. . . .

Second, the anointing of the sick is a privileged liturgical expression of ecclesial care and mission of the community. The scriptural passage that is usually cited to justify anointing is James 5:14–15, in which the writer reminds his readers of an already existing custom in the church. When there are sick in the Christian community, the leaders anoint them with oil and pray for them. The promised effects are their being "raised up" and having their sins forgiven. Behind this pastoral care of the sick is an implicit theology that God always touches the whole person in healing and that the community in doing this ministry imitates Christ. (The scriptural connection of physical healing and forgiveness exemplifies this conviction.) This ministry of the local community to the sick is liturgically concretized when the sick are brought the eucharist directly from the Sunday celebration by deputed members and when anointing is celebrated communally.

> **The Paschal Mystery**
>
> The Paschal Mystery is the work of salvation accomplished by Jesus Christ mainly through his life, Passion, death, Resurrection, and Ascension. This is the ultimate source of hope for Christians. In Jesus, God gave himself to suffering and death. If we unite our life and death with Jesus, we will rise from the dead as he rose from the dead.

Theology also provides a word of caution for this ministry. The sick are not healed for their private purposes but to fulfill their role within the larger mission of the church to the world. The Second Vatican Council urges the sick to show their concern for the whole people of God "by associating themselves freely with the passion and death of Christ" (*Lumen Gentium* 11). In contrast to an individualistic concept of the sacrament, the Christian's strengthening in the life of Christ cannot be separated from the work of Christ. Even the Christian's sickness should provide a witness to the transforming effect of the **paschal mystery** in human life.

Finally, the calling down of the Holy Spirit, with the forgiveness of sins proper to anointing, enriches our understanding and experience of the forgiveness first extended in the initiating sacraments and then penance and reconciliation. All adult sacramental participation presupposes a faith that is the first fruit of God's justifying work in us. In the sacramental ministry of the church, this faith is proclaimed in a privileged symbolic act. But these sacramentally expressed acts of faith always implicitly are a plea for God's continuing and enabling healing. The sacramental form of anointing captures this plea: "Through this holy anointing may the Lord in His love and mercy help you with the grace of the Holy Spirit. May the Lord who frees you from sin save you and raise you up."[1]

Erik Erikson has suggested that the final task of the human person before death is integrity, literally "making a whole" of our lives. Sickness and death are to be counted among the ultimate limit—experiences from which we will either wring new meaning for our lives or put in jeopardy the search for such integrity. Within the Christian perspective, since Christ is the Alpha and Omega, the beginning and the end (as the Easter liturgy beautifully phrases it), both integrity and limit-experience are radically transformed. For two thousand years members of the Christian communities have pondered the meaning of the paschal mystery so that their own lives and death have meaning. All the Christian traditions, whether they counted anointing of the sick among the sacraments or not, have shaped ministries and liturgies to help Christians profit from such experiences. For ultimately, eschatology is not a theological notion but an experience shaped by the praxis of our lives and limitations.

Endnote

1. *Pastoral Care*, no. 3 (in *Documents on the Liturgy 1963–1979*, no. 6).

Excerpt from "Rest Assured: The Anointing of the Sick"

By John Shea

Alan Williamson was in his late 50s and had been fighting cancer for more than eight years. His wife, Jean, was a quiet presence at his side. They had three daughters, Corrie, Cindy, and Matty. Corrie and Matty were married. Cindy, the middle one, was shy. She never said much.

As the elevator opened on seven, Corrie was standing there.

"Could I talk with you, Father?" Without waiting for an answer, she continued, "Dr. Schwartz tells us Daddy's pain medication is not working as well as it did. He says he can sedate him, but he will be out of it. I think that means he would die in his sleep, just slip away." Tears suddenly filled her eyes. "I don't know what we should do or how to talk to Daddy about it. I don't want him to suffer, but . . ." Her voice trailed off and she dabbed her eyes with a Kleenex that had been crumpled in her hand.

"Let's walk down to the room. I think it is best we all talk openly with one another," [Father] Charlie said. "You know, we are all dying, not just your father."

Corrie did not know this. She stood still and said nothing. Charlie took her hand and walked a few steps, almost pulling her behind him. She might have been a little girl being pulled along on an adult adventure. Then he let go of her hand and they walked side by side.

The first bed in Room 718 was unoccupied. Alan was in the second. He was surrounded by technological medicine—oxygen in his nose, multiple drips in his arms, a catheter for urine. His eyelids were heavy, but he was talking and making sense. When he saw the old priest enter the room, he reached up his hand. Charlie took it. At the same time his wife, Jean, clasped Charlie's other hand.

"Thanks for coming, Father. This means a lot to us," Jean said.

Alan nodded. "We did it before in church. Guess it didn't take," Alan wheezed. His voice was labored and painfully slow. All he could manage was a smile at his little joke. Everyone else was grateful to be able to laugh.

The old priest had seen it many times: the dying comforting the living by joking and talking about "business as usual." Especially parents. They instinctively protected their children. This became one last way they tried to shield them.

"Well, we'll have to do it till we get it right," Charlie went along with the game. "We've got all the right people. We're all here." He looked around at Jean and the daughters and two of their husbands. Then he turned to the bed. "All the people who love you, Alan. We are here with you and we are not leaving."

"Good," said Alan.

"Let's begin," said Charlie. "Let's gather. I'll guide us as we go along."

The priest greeted everybody with peace and prayed that God would be present to Alan and everyone Alan loves in this difficult time of dying. Whatever frivolity was in the room left. Everyone was silent.

Dr. Schwartz and Alice entered the room.

"Just in time[,]" Charlie said, "We're just beginning. Enter the circle."

"This woman is a saint," Alan said softly. He meant Alice. She had cared for him in his two previous hospital stays, and they had become friends.

"You're not too bad either, Dr. Schwartz," Matty said.

Everyone laughed.

"I'm used to second fiddle," shrugged Jacob Schwartz.

More laughter.

"Hardly," said Alice and rolled her eyes in such a way that everyone knew the doctor is always in charge.

More laughter.

"There's a penance rite here begging to be said," interrupted Charlie. "Whenever I say, 'Lord, have mercy,' say it back to me." There was silence once again.

"Lord, you are present to us in times of affliction. Lord, have mercy."

A weak "Lord, have mercy" came back at Charlie.

"Lord, you forgive us our sins. Christ, have mercy."

Everyone responded "Christ, have mercy," even Dr. Schwartz, who was Jewish.

"Lord Jesus, your death brings us to life. Lord, have mercy."

The "Lord, have mercy" came back a little stronger.

Now there was real silence, a silence pregnant with a word. The people were gathered. . . .

"You taught us so much, Daddy. Now you are teaching us how to die," said Matty.

"I'd just as soon not," said her father.

Then after a long pause he said, "Wait a minute." Alan closed his eyes. He seemed to be gathering strength from somewhere inside. Obediently, everyone waited.

"I want to make sure everyone is OK. I worry for you," the dying father finally said.

"We're OK, Daddy." Corrie looked around to get everyone's support.

Alan held up his index and middle finger and crossed them. He was getting too weak for speech but not for hope. . . .

"I am going to lay my hands on you, Alan, and I want you to touch me back," Charlie said. "Then I am going to ask everyone else to do the same. It is an ancient ritual."

The old priest laid his hands on Alan's head. Then he picked up Alan's hand and put it on his head. Alan pushed down a bit. It was more than a touch, almost a squeeze. Charlie smiled.

The old priest moved away from Alan. He went over to Bed 1, sat down, and watched. Everyone else moved in on Alan. The laying on of hands became touching and hugging and crying and saying, "I love you." The sons-in-law were awkward. They touched Alan and then put their arms around their wives. Alice and Dr. Schwartz laid their hands on Alan without a medical reason, without probing for a problem or trying to soothe a pain. Jean laid her head on his chest. Alan ran his hands over them all, touched their faces, rubbed their arms, clasped their hands. To the eyes of the old priest there was no greediness in Alan's hands. He said a prayer to God for the knowing ways of touch.

Then suddenly Charlie thought about his own death and who would be touching him. He had outlived many of his friends, and the ones who were still alive might not be able to come. Unless his nephews flew in, it would probably be Sister Terry, the interpreter of sleep, and the other chaplains. Then again, he thought, I may konk out quickly. Who knows? Death plays no favorites.

Everyone was quieting down. Charlie pushed himself off the bed and joined the circle. "Alan, we would like to anoint you and assure you of God's love."

Charlie opened the book, anointed Alan's forehead, and read the words slowly.

"Through this holy anointing may the Lord in his love and mercy help you with the grace of the Holy Spirit. . . . Amen."

Then he anointed his hands and said, "May the Lord who frees you from sin save you and raise you up. . . . Amen."

Then the old priest continued: "Lord Jesus Christ, you chose to share our human nature, to redeem all people, and to heal the sick. Look with compassion upon your servant, Alan, whom we have anointed in your name with this holy oil for the healing of his body and spirit. Support him with your power, comfort him with your protection, and give him the strength to fight against evil. Since you have given him a share in your own Passion, help him to find hope in suffering, for you are Lord forever and ever." Cindy said, "Amen."

Charlie took out the pyx. He had forgotten to take it out earlier. It contained ten consecrated hosts. He raised one up and said in utter amazement, "This is the bread of life. Taste and see that the Lord is good."

He put the host in front of Alan's eyes and said, "Body of Christ."

A hoarse "Amen" came from Alan. . . .

Alan received the Body of Christ. Charlie asked Jean to give him some water. Then he distributed Holy Communion to all who were willing to receive it. Dr. Schwartz shook his head no.

Then Charlie asked everyone to sit or lean against the wall—to get comfortable—and spend some time in silent communion with God and with each other. . . .

The old priest had come to believe strange things about Communion. He felt people were together in deep spiritual ways, ways deeper than physical touch and ways that surpassed physical passing. He did not believe the next world was separate from this world but a different dimension of it. . . . "Nothing can separate us from the love of God made visible in Christ Jesus our Lord." His favorite quote. So simple, yet it takes a lifetime to realize. . . .

The old priest knew there was one more prayer to say and the ritual would be over. But he was in no hurry to say it. He was in no hurry to rush from these open fields. So he stayed there—with Alan in the center and Jean next to him, with Corrie, Cindy, and Matty, with Dr. Schwartz and Alice, and with the two sons-in-law, whose names he had forgotten. They all stayed there together—seemingly in a place just right—honoring love by being vigilant as life passes.

For Reflection

1. In the second reading, Regis A. Duffy says there are two communal aspects to the Sacrament of Anointing of the Sick. First, it expresses the Church's care for the sick person; second, the sick person serves the community. Explain how a seriously ill person can serve the community.

2. Do you believe God can physically heal someone? Explain.

3. The story by John Shea says, "The old priest had come to believe strange things about Communion. He felt people were together in deep spiritual ways, ways deeper than physical touch and ways that surpassed physical passing. He did not believe the next world was separate from this world but a different dimension of it." Do you agree with this statement? Explain. If possible, reflect on whether you have experienced this kind of spiritual communion and closeness with those who have passed.

4. The second reading indicates there are three aspects to Anointing of the Sick: being united to Christ's sufferings, being communally connected, and receiving forgiveness. How do you see these three aspects in the story by John Shea?

Part 4

The Sacraments at the Service of Communion

15 The Baptismal Call to Holiness and Service

Introduction

Two of the Seven Sacraments of the Catholic Church, the Sacrament of Holy Orders and the Sacrament of Matrimony, are designated as Sacraments for the service of the community and are called the **Sacraments at the Service of Communion**. Chapter 2 addressed the offer of salvation as a call to enter into a relationship of intimacy with God the Father and with his people through Jesus Christ. It is a call to communion. Holy Orders and Matrimony are Sacraments that are to bring about this communion.

The Second Vatican Council wanted to recover that which is essential to the Sacraments and to bring new expression to these essential truths. The Church as mystical communion is a deep truth that the Church wanted to have at the forefront of the minds of the faithful. In the past, although there had always been a deeper communal understanding of Holy Orders and Matrimony, sometimes these and other Sacraments were perceived and practiced as private acts. For example, it was standard practice for priests to offer "private Masses," at which no one else was present. Furthermore, marriage was perceived as a lesser call than a call to the priesthood or religious life. Priests were the ones seen as doing the work of ministry; others were seen as the recipients of ministry.

". . . All the faithful of Christ are invited to strive for the holiness and perfection of their

Sacraments at the Service of Communion Two Sacraments (the Sacraments of Holy Orders and Matrimony) that bestow the grace and strength to serve others in love within and through the Church community.

own proper state" (*Dogmatic Constitution on the Church* [*Lumen Gentium*], 42). With this phrase, the Church declares that every baptized person is called to holiness. When one is baptized into Jesus Christ, that person is baptized into Jesus' mission of salvation. Drawing all people into intimacy with God and God's people is the ministry of all baptized people, not just priests and religious.

The call to holiness and the call to ministry cannot remain abstract ideals. These calls need to be lived in concrete ways. In this chapter's readings, the Church offers, to priests and to all Christians, a vision of life as an embrace of the call to holiness.

The first reading, from *Lumen Gentium*, reminds us that people must seek to be holy in whatever state of life they find themselves: single, married, ordained, or vowed religious. In the second reading, Pope John Paul II urges the young people of the world not to assume that marriage is a "default" way of living. He encourages young people to be intentional about their lives and to seek God's will for their vocation. Marriage is a vocation that is to be intentionally entered into because God has a great purpose for marriage to serve the world and to announce the Gospel. Finally, in the readings from the third part of the chapter, a seminarian shares his story of discernment and a college professor, married with children, encourages us to reflect on the meaning of marriage and its future.

Excerpt from "The Universal Call to Holiness in the Church," from *Dogmatic Constitution on the Church (Lumen Gentium)*

By the Second Vatican Council

40. The Lord Jesus, the divine Teacher and Model of all perfection, preached holiness of life to each and everyone of His disciples of every condition. He Himself stands as the author and consummator of this holiness of life: "Be you therefore perfect, even as your heavenly Father is perfect." (Mt. 5:48) Indeed He sent the Holy Spirit upon all men that He

> ### The Shepherds of Christ's Flock
>
> The Church's bishops and priests are entrusted with the care of the members of the Church, as a shepherd cares for a flock of sheep.

might move them inwardly to love God with their whole heart and their whole soul, with all their mind and all their strength (Cf. Mk. 12:30) and that they might love each other as Christ loves them. (Cf. Jn. 13:34; 15:12) The followers of Christ are called by God, not because of their works, but according to His own purpose and grace. They are justified in the Lord Jesus, because in the baptism of faith they truly become sons of God and sharers in the divine nature. In this way they are really made holy. Then too, by God's gift, they must hold on to and complete in their lives this holiness they have received. They are warned by the Apostle to live "as becomes saints," (Eph. 5:3) and to put on "as God's chosen ones, holy and beloved a heart of mercy, kindness, humility, meekness, patience," (Col. 3:12) and to possess the fruit of the Spirit in holiness. (Cf. Gal. 5:22; Rom. 6:22) Since truly we all offend in many things (Cf. Jas. 3:2) we all need God's mercies continually and we all must daily pray: "Forgive us our debts."(1 Mt. 6:12) . . .

41. . . . In the first place, the shepherds of Christ's flock must holily and eagerly, humbly and courageously carry out their ministry, in imitation of the eternal high Priest, the Shepherd and Guardian of our souls. They ought to fulfill this duty in such a way that it will be the principal means also of their own sanctification. Those chosen for the fullness of the priesthood are granted the ability of exercising the perfect duty of pastoral charity by the grace of the sacrament of Orders. This perfect duty of pastoral charity is exercised in every form of episcopal care and service, prayer, sacrifice and preaching. By this same sacramental grace, they are given the courage necessary to lay down their lives for their sheep, and the ability of promoting greater holiness in the Church by their daily example, having become a pattern for their flock (Cf. 1 Pt. 5:3). . . .

> ### The Fullness of the Priesthood
>
> Deacons and presbyters (priests) are ordained, but the fullness of the priesthood is in the episcopacy, the bishops.

Furthermore, married couples and Christian parents should follow their own proper path (to holiness) by faithful love. They should sustain one another in grace throughout the entire length of their lives. They should embue their offspring, lovingly welcomed as God's gift, with Christian doctrine and the evangelical virtues. In this manner, they offer all men the example of unwearying and generous love; in this way they build up the brotherhood of charity; in so doing, they stand as the witnesses and cooperators in the fruitfulness of Holy Mother Church; by such lives, they are a sign and a participation in that very love, with which Christ loved His Bride and for which He delivered Himself up for her.[1] A like example, but one given in a different way, is that offered by widows and single people, who are able to make great contributions toward holiness and apostolic endeavor in the Church. Finally, those who engage in labor—and frequently it is of a heavy nature—should better themselves by their human labors. They should be of aid to their fellow citizens. They should raise all of society, and even creation itself, to a better

> 66 *Married couples and Christian parents should follow their own proper path (to holiness) by faithful love. They should sustain one another in grace throughout the entire length of their lives.* 99

mode of existence. Indeed, they should imitate by their lively charity, in their joyous hope and by their voluntary sharing of each others' burdens, the very Christ who plied His hands with carpenter's tools and Who in union with His Father, is continually working for the salvation of all men. In this, then, their daily work they should climb to the heights of holiness and apostolic activity. . . .

Finally all Christ's faithful, whatever be the conditions, duties and circumstances of their lives—and indeed through all these, will daily increase in holiness, if they receive all things with faith from the hand of their heavenly Father and if they cooperate with the divine will. In this temporal service, they will manifest to all men the love with which God loved the world.

42. "God is love, and he who abides in love, abides in God and God in Him." (1 Jn. 4:16) But, God pours out his love into our hearts through

the Holy Spirit, Who has been given to us; (Cf. Rom. 5:5) thus the first and most necessary gift is love, by which we love God above all things and our neighbor because of God. Indeed, in order that love, as good seed[,] may grow and bring forth fruit in the soul, each one of the faithful must willingly hear the Word of God and accept His Will, and must complete what God has begun by their own actions with the help of God's grace. These actions consist in the use of the sacraments and in a special way the Eucharist, frequent participation in the sacred action of the Liturgy, application of oneself to prayer, self-abnegation, lively fraternal service and the constant exercise of all the virtues. For charity, as the bond of perfection and the fullness of the law, (Cf. Col. 3:14; Rom. 13:10) rules over all the means of attaining holiness and gives life to these same means. It is charity which guides us to our final end. It is the love of God and the love of one's neighbor which points out the true disciple of Christ. . . .

Therefore, all the faithful of Christ are invited to strive for the holiness and perfection of their own proper state. Indeed they have an obligation to so strive. Let all then have care that they guide aright their own deepest sentiments of soul. Let neither the use of the things of this world nor attachment to riches, which is against the spirit of evangelical poverty, hinder them in their quest for perfect love[.] Let them heed the admonition of the Apostle to those who use this world; let them not come to terms with this world; for this world, as we see it, is passing away. (Cf[.] 1 Cor. 7:31 ff.)

Endnote

1. Pius XI, Litt. Encycl. Casti Connubii, 31 Dec. 1930. AAS 22 (1930) p. 548 s. Cfr. S. Io Chrysostomus, In Ephes. Hom. 20, 2: P. 62, 136 ss.

Excerpt from "Apostolic Letter, *Dilecti Amici*, of Pope John Paul II to the Youth of the World on the Occasion of International Youth Year"

By Pope Saint John Paul II

8. . . . At this moment, however, I wish to speak to you about the particular meaning of the words which Christ said to the young man [who asked Jesus what he must do to inherit eternal life]. And I do this in the conviction that Christ addresses them in the Church to some of his young questioners in every generation. In ours too. His words therefore signify a particular vocation in the community of the People of God. The Church finds Christ's "Follow me" (Cf. Mk 10:21; Jn 1:43; 21:29) at the beginning of every call to service in the ministerial priesthood, which simultaneously in the Catholic Church of the Latin Rite is linked to the conscious and free choice of celibacy. The Church finds the same "follow me" of Christ at the beginning of the religious vocation, whereby, through the profession of the evangelical counsels (chastity, poverty and obedience), a man or woman recognizes as his or her own the programme of life which Christ himself lived on earth, for the sake of the Kingdom of God. (Cf. Mt 19:12) By professing religious vows, such individuals commit themselves to bearing a particular witness to the love of God above all things, and likewise to that call to union with God in eternity which is directed to everyone. But there is a need for some to bear an exceptional witness to this before other people. . . .

It is for this reason that I wish to say this to all of you young people, in this important phase of the development of your personality as a man or a woman: if such a call comes into your heart, do not silence it! Let it develop into the maturity of a vocation! Respond to it through prayer and fidelity to the commandments! For "the harvest is plentiful" (Mt. 9:3, 7) and there is an enormous need for many to be reached by Christ's call "Follow me." There is an enormous need for priests according to the heart of God—and the Church and the world of today have an enormous need of the witness of a life given without reserve to God: the witness of that nuptial love of Christ himself which in a particular way will make the Kingdom of God present among people and bring it nearer to the world. . . .

"Pray therefore the Lord of the harvest to send out labourers into his harvest," (Mt 9:37) continues Christ. And these words, especially in our times, become a programme of prayer and action for more priestly and religious vocations. With this programme the Church addresses herself to you, to youth. And you too: pray! And if the fruit of this prayer of the Church comes to life in the depths of your heart, listen to the Master as he says: "Follow me." . . .

9. . . . Here it should be noted that in the period before the Second Vatican Council the concept of "vocation" was applied first of all to the priesthood and religious life, as if Christ had addressed to the young person his evangelical "Follow me" only for these cases. The Council has broadened this way of looking at things. Priestly and religious vocations have kept their particular character and their sacramental and charismatic importance in the life of the People of God. But at the same time the awareness renewed by the Second Vatican Council of the universal sharing of all the baptized in Christ's three-fold prophetic, priestly and kingly mission, (tria munera), as also the awareness of the universal vocation to holiness,[1] have led to a realization of the fact that every human life vocation, as a Christian vocation, corresponds to the evangelical call. Christ's "Follow me" makes itself heard on the different paths taken by the disciples and confessors of the divine Redeemer. There are different ways of becoming imitators of Christ—not only by bearing witness to the **eschatological Kingdom** of truth and love, but also by striving to bring about the transformation of the whole of temporal reality according to the spirit of the Gospel.[2] It is at this point that there also begins the apostolate of the laity, which is inseparable from the very essence of the Christian vocation. . . .

eschatological Kingdom Eschatology is the study of the end times or "the last things": the Last Judgment, the particular judgment, the resurrection of the body, Heaven, Hell, and Purgatory. The eschatological Kingdom is the day when God's Reign comes in its fullness.

You must also rethink—and very profoundly—the meaning of Baptism and Confirmation. For in these two sacraments is contained the fundamental deposit of the Christian life and vocation. From these there begins the path towards the Eucharist, which contains the fullness of the sacramental gifts granted to the Christian: all the Church's spiritual wealth is concentrated in this Sacrament of love. It is also necessary—and always in relationship with the Eucharist—to reflect on the Sacrament of Penance, which is of irreplaceable importance for the formation of the Christian personality, especially if it is linked with spiritual direction, which is a systematic school of the interior life. . . .

> 66 *There is an enormous need for priests according to the heart of God—and the Church and the world of today have an enormous need of the witness of a life given without reserve to God: the witness of that nuptial love of Christ himself which in a particular way will make the Kingdom of God present among people and bring it nearer to the world.* 99

The Church herself—as the Second Vatican Council teaches—is "a kind of sacrament or sign of intimate union with God, and of the unity of all mankind."[3] Every vocation in life, insofar as it is a "Christian" vocation, is rooted in the sacramentality of the Church: it is therefore formed through the Sacraments of our faith. The Sacraments enable us from our youth to open our human "I" to the saving action of God, that is, of the Most Blessed Trinity. They enable us to share in God's life, living the authentic human life to the full. In this way our human life acquires a new dimension and at the same time its Christian originality: awareness of the demands placed on man by the Gospel is matched by awareness of the gift which surpasses everything. "If you knew the gift of God," (Jn 4:10) said Christ, speaking to the Samaritan woman.

10. Against this vast background that your youthful plan of life acquires in relation to the idea of the Christian vocation, I wish to examine, together with you young people to whom I am addressing this Letter, the question that in a certain sense is at the heart of the youth of all of you. This is one of the central questions of human life, and at the same time one of the central themes of reflection, creativity and culture. It is also one of the main biblical themes, and one to which I personally have devoted much reflection and analysis. God created human beings: male and female, thereby introducing into the history of the human race that special "duality" together with complete equality, in the matter of human dignity;

> **Complementarity**
>
> Pope John Paul II provided a new way to understand the human person through his "theology of the body." Part of that theology is a theology of marriage, based on the way male and female complete each other.

and with marvelous complementarity, in the matter of the division of the attributes, properties and tasks linked with the masculinity and femininity of the human being. . . .

In each separate case all of this has its own unrepeatable subjective expression, its affective richness, indeed its **metaphysical beauty**. At the same time, in all of this there is contained a powerful exhortation not to distort this expression, not to destroy this treasure and not to disfigure this beauty. Be convinced that this call comes from God himself, who created man "in his own image and likeness" precisely "as man and woman." This call flows from the Gospel and makes itself heard in the voice of young consciences, if they have preserved their simplicity and purity: "Blessed are the pure in heart, for they shall see God." (Mt 5:8) Yes, through that love which is born in you—and wishes to become a part of your whole plan of life—you must see God who is love. (Cf. 1 Jn 4:8, 16). . . .

To set out on the path of the married vocation means to learn married love day by day, year by year: love according to soul and body, love that "is patient, is kind, that does not insist on its own way . . . and does not rejoice at wrong": love that "rejoices in the right," love that "endures all things." (Cf. 1 Cor 13:4, 5, 6, 7)

It is precisely this love that you young people need if your married future is to "pass the test" of the whole of life. And precisely this test is part of the very essence of the vocation which, through marriage, you intend to include in the plan of your life. . . .

metaphysical beauty The beauty of the human person that cannot be seen by the human eye.

Endnotes

1. Cf. Second Vatican Council, *Dogmatic Constitution on the Church (Lumen Gentium)*, 39–42.
2. Cf. Second Vatican Council, *Pastoral Constitution on the Church in the Modern World (Gaudium et Spes)*, 43–44.
3. Second Vatican Council, *Dogmatic Constitution on the Church (Lumen Gentium)*, 1.

Excerpt from "Vocation Story,"
By Gale Hammerschmidt

Why am I studying to become a priest? This is not necessarily an easy question to answer. It is also not a question that I feel I can answer with one hundred percent certainty. As I look back on my journey it seems clear to me that God has played a larger role in getting me to this point than I have.

. . . I have two wonderful parents, and I have three great sisters. As a youngster I went to church every weekend, attended religious education classes, and was a pretty good kid. I attended [Catholic] school, and I was filled with a solid knowledge of the Church. After I graduated high school . . . I attended . . . university. Although I still went to church almost every weekend, it would be a lie to say that I continued to keep God at the center of my life. Through college and even a few years after I had graduated from college, I allowed my own selfishness to lead me into making a number of bad decisions. These decisions, and the emptiness I felt after making such decisions made me realize exactly how much I needed God to be the focal point of my life.

I was very blessed by the fact that after I had graduated from [college] . . . I was able to obtain [a] teaching position. . . . While in the midst of thinking mostly about myself and what I wanted, I was being surrounded by people who were helping me realize that life was not just about my own personal desires. I was introduced to Eucharistic adoration . . . and I began to spend an hour a week in silence simply being in the presence of our Lord. I soon came to look forward to this hour and I realized how God had the ability to transform all things. . . .

It still amazes me how much joy living your life for God can bring. During these past four years practically every aspect of my life has changed. I have made many new friends, I look forward to attending daily mass, I pray more, and I have realized that God knows exactly what makes me happy. Things that I used to think were important have become less important, and my life has been transformed before my very eyes. I can remember . . . when I won a local golf tournament, and I remembered thinking to myself, "Is this it? Is this all the joy that comes from such an accomplishment?" The one thing that would have made me so happy in the past seemed so trivial now. It had become clear to me that living a life for God was the greatest joy.

. . . I became even more involved in the church, and my love for the Catholic faith really started to take shape. Every time I would question the faith, I would find that the Church was solid. It was also at this time that I started to realize that my potential calling to the priesthood should not be ignored. I began to talk to people about it, and I started to receive some good advice. I realized that I would never know for sure if God is calling me to the priesthood unless I went to the seminary to find out. I was moved by a story of a guy who had even broken off his wedding engagement because he simply needed to find out if God was calling him to the priesthood before he could feel comfortable getting married. I even spoke with a few people who had attended the seminary and then decided it wasn't for them. Through these conversations I realized that there was no shame in giving it a shot regardless of the outcome.

I guess this brings me to where I am now. At the age of thirty-three, I am in the process of beginning my first year as a seminarian. I feel that I am taking a courageous step, and I am excited to see where it leads. I know that there are many people in my life who have doubts about what I am doing, and at times I have the same doubts. I am leaving a life that I have absolutely loved, and I have such fond memories of the times I have spent with my students. I have also never been far from my family. These are some of the things that make me anxious, and I wonder if my life as a priest will be able to provide me with the same amount of joy as my previous life has. I also at times worry about the thought of never getting married. I really believe that I could be very happy as a husband and a father.

Ultimately, though, I don't spend much of my time worrying over such things. I realize that worrying is pointless, and I do have a tremendous amount of trust in the Lord. As I mentioned earlier; He has not let me down in the past and I know that He will not let me down in the future. In the end I gain strength by focusing on the fact that everything I have was given to me by God, and that my life is in His hands.

Excerpt from "The Future of Marriage,"
by Natalie Kertes Weaver, PhD

From many accounts, marriage is in crisis. Poverty threatens families throughout the world, and the most vulnerable families are those in which marriage is not even present, that is, single-parent households. Teenage pregnancy is rising and becoming more socially acceptable, even while it puts children and their children at risk. It is increasingly common for couples to choose to live together before marriage, which statistically puts them at higher risk of divorce after marriage. . . . Couples marry later in life than ever before, and many cohabiting couples choose not to marry. Culturally relaxed attitudes toward premarital, extramarital, and nonmarital sex suggest that people will delay marriage if they marry at all. One in four households is unsafe due to domestic violence.

Changing economic realities give couples, and particularly women, more freedom in marriage than ever before. People no longer have to stay in bad marriages because of financial need. Moreover, changing understandings of personhood, driven by new studies in gender, psychology, biology, and philosophy, have uprooted the traditional, patriarchal model of family life. . . . Nontraditional models of family life are explored, particularly by same-sex couples seeking legal marriage as both an option and a legal right.

All this change has resulted in an upheaval of marriage and its dependability as a social reality. People ask themselves why they should marry, especially when marriage so often appears to be a liability to personal freedom, safety, and happiness. Persons denied marriage, such as same-sex couples, see the inability to marry legally as discrimination, as they view marriage as the ultimate gateway to full social recognition and participation.

In helping to negotiate such questions and crises facing contemporary marriages, it is helpful to remember that the future of marriage as a function of society may also be viewed from an eschatological perspective. . . . What role does marriage play in societal human flourishing? What role does marriage play in the realization of social justice, human dignity, authentic charity, and freedom within society as a whole? One's view of the good of marriage and laws that surround marriage should be formed in relationship to an understanding of marriage as it relates to the common welfare. Is marriage an integral part of society? Should it be? How should it be? Why? Does it reflect the values of the Kingdom of God? Can I define my understanding of these values and place marriage within them?

. . . I would argue that unreflective marriage benefits no one. The passion of sexual attraction wears off over time, and the daily tasks of laundry, dishes, work, and diapers can become boring if not hated. Hostility, frustration, and a general sense of "I could have done better" can lead people into marital decline, complete with feelings of powerlessness and suffocation.

On the other hand, reflective marriage . . . is a gift and an opportunity. Such a marriage is lived deliberately and is attached to the deepest sense of one's purpose and personal value. Marriage that strives to be covenant and sacrament, marriage that strives to realize dignity and justice, marriage that manifests itself in charity and holy union, marriage that transmits life to children and kin and neighbor is a prophetic stance against all the worst in society and an affirmation of all that is possible in human relationships. Such a marriage represents the possibility of the real becoming the ideal.

For Reflection

1. *Lumen Gentium* says all Christians are called to holiness in accordance with their state in life. As a student, what three things might you do to respond to the call to holiness?

2. This chapter's readings indicate that no vocation is an accident. It is to be intentional. Right now, to what vocation do you feel called? Explain.

3. Holy Orders and Matrimony are designated as Sacraments at the Service of Communion. How do you think the Sacrament of Matrimony can announce God's offer of salvation and so serve the Church and the world?

16 The Sacrament of Holy Orders

Introduction

To understand the priesthood, we must first understand the ministry and the person of the **bishop**. You will notice this explanation in the chapter's first reading, from *Dogmatic Constitution on the Church (Lumen Gentium)*. This selection begins its explanation of the **Sacrament of Holy Orders** with the ministry of the bishop in whom the "fullness" of the priesthood rests. The first "priest" of any diocese or archdiocese is the office of the **episcopate**, or bishop. The presence of the Eucharist, the teaching of sound doctrine, the governance of Church matters, and the pastoral care of the people in a diocese: all of these depend on the presence of the bishop. To assist the bishop in these ministries, he ordains assistants to the priesthood, also known as the order of the presbyterate. Priests assist the bishop by preaching the Word, presiding at the Eucharist, and administering other Sacraments. Also assisting the bishop are **deacons**, who can witness marriages, preside at funerals, serve as ministers of the Word, and especially serve the needy in their communities. The fullness

bishop One who has received the fullness of the Sacrament of Holy Orders and is a successor to the Apostles.

Sacrament of Holy Orders The Sacrament by which members of the Church are ordained for permanent ministry in the Church as bishops, priests, or deacons.

episcopate The office, or order, of bishop.

deacon One who is ordained for service and ministry, but not for ministerial priesthood, through the Sacrament of Holy Orders. Deacons are ordained to assist priests and bishops in a variety of liturgical and charitable ministries.

of pastoral ministry rests with the bishop, while he entrusts priests and deacons to assist in his ministry.

In chapter 15, the readings focused on the universal call to holiness and to the importance of marriage as a vocation. This was to emphasize the call for holy marriages. Marriage is elevated, but the priesthood is not diminished. Saint John Chrysostom (347–407) gives us our second reading. He is one of the "patristic writers," or Church Fathers. These writers hold a unique place in Catholic and Orthodox theology, and their writings hold a particular authority. Because of this, it is important that we know what they say. Chrysostom wrote extensively about the priesthood and the great dignity priests have. For example, Chrysostom says that priests are "the authors of our birth from God."

Our chapter's final reading, however, teaches that the priesthood is not a place of privilege in human terms. We hear from a man who became a priest under difficult circumstances. You will see that during his five years of seminary study, the seminary moved three times to avoid government persecution.

In all these readings, you see the greatness of the call to priestly ministry. Service, sacrifice, and sanctity are intimately linked with the call. God has entrusted much to the priestly office and demands much in return.

Excerpt from *Dogmatic Constitution on the Church (Lumen Gentium)*

By the Second Vatican Council

18. For the nurturing and constant growth of the People of God, Christ the Lord instituted in His Church a variety of ministries, which work for the good of the whole body. For those ministers, who are endowed with sacred power, serve their brethren, so that all who are of the People of God, and therefore enjoy a true Christian dignity, working toward a common goal freely and in an orderly way, may arrive at salvation. . . .

20. That divine mission, entrusted by Christ to the apostles, will last until the end of the world, (cf. Mt. 28:20) since the Gospel they are to teach is for all time the source of all life for the Church. And for this reason the apostles, appointed as rulers in this society, took care to appoint successors.

For they not only had helpers in their ministry, but also, in order that the mission assigned to them might continue after their death, they passed on to their immediate cooperators, as it were, in the form of a testament, the duty of confirming and finishing the work begun by themselves, recommending to them that they attend to the whole flock in which the Holy Spirit placed them to shepherd the Church of God. (Cf. Acts 20:28.) They therefore appointed such men, and gave them the order that, when they should have died, other approved men would take up their ministry. Among those various ministries which, according to tradition, were exercised in the Church from the earliest times, the chief place belongs to the office of those who, appointed to the episcopate, by a succession running from the beginning, are passers-on of the apostolic seed. Thus, as St. Irenaeus testifies, through those who were appointed bishops by the apostles, and through their successors down in our own time, the apostolic tradition is manifested and preserved.

Bishops, therefore, with their helpers, the priests and deacons, have taken up the service of the community, presiding in place of God over the flock, whose shepherds they are, as teachers for doctrine, priests for sacred worship, and ministers for governing. . . . Therefore, the Sacred Council teaches that bishops by divine institution have succeeded to the place of the apostles, as shepherds of the Church, and he who hears them, hears Christ, and he who rejects them, rejects Christ and Him who sent Christ. (Cf. Lk.

> ### Successors to the Apostles
>
> The Second Vatican Council reminds the Church of the beginnings of the ministry of the bishop. The Apostles founded churches and then appointed bishops to continue their ministry after they left to found other churches. This term is directly related to the term *apostolic succession*: The uninterrupted passing on of apostolic preaching and authority from the Apostles directly to all bishops, accomplished through the laying on of hands in the Sacrament of Holy Orders.

10:16.)

21. In the bishops, therefore, for whom priests are assistants, Our Lord Jesus Christ, the Supreme High Priest, is present in the midst of those who believe. For sitting at the right hand of God the Father, He is not absent from the gathering of His high priests, but above all through their excellent service He is preaching the word of God to all nations, and constantly administering the sacraments of faith to those who believe, by their

> *Bishops, therefore, with their helpers, the priests and deacons, have taken up the service of the community, presiding in place of God over the flock, whose shepherds they are, as teachers for doctrine, priests for sacred worship, and ministers for governing.*

paternal functioning. (Cf. 1 Cor. 4:15.) He incorporates new members in His Body by a heavenly regeneration, and finally by their wisdom and prudence He directs and guides the People of the New Testament in their pilgrimage toward eternal happiness. These pastors, chosen to shepherd the Lord's flock of the elect, are servants of Christ and stewards of the mysteries of God, (cf. 1 Cor. 4:1) to whom has been assigned the bearing of witness to the Gospel of the grace of God, (cf. Rom. 15:15; Acts 20:24) and the ministration of the Spirit and of justice in glory. (Cf. 2 Cor. 3:8–9.)

For the discharging of such great duties, the apostles were enriched by Christ with a special outpouring of the Holy Spirit coming upon them, (cf. Acts 1:8, 2:4, Jn. 20:22–23) and they passed on this spiritual gift to their helpers by the imposition of hands, (cf. 1 Tim. 4:14; 2 Tim. 1:6–7) and it has been transmitted down to us in Episcopal consecration. And the Sacred Council teaches that by Episcopal consecration the fullness of the sacrament of Orders is conferred, that fullness of power, namely, which both in the Church's liturgical practice and in the language of the Fathers of the Church is called the high priesthood, the supreme power of the sacred ministry. . . .

28. Christ, whom the Father has sanctified and sent into the world, (Jn. 10:36) has through His apostles, made their successors, the bishops, partakers of His consecration and His mission. They have legitimately

handed on to different individuals in the Church various degrees of participation in this ministry. Thus the divinely established ecclesiastical ministry is exercised on different levels by those who from antiquity have been called bishops, priests and deacons. Priests, although they do not possess the highest degree of the priesthood, and although they are dependent on the bishops in the exercise of their power, nevertheless they are united with the bishops in **sacerdotal** dignity. By the power of the sacrament of Orders, in the image of Christ the eternal high Priest, (Heb. 5:1–10, 7:24, 9:11–28) they are consecrated to preach the Gospel and shepherd the faithful and to celebrate divine worship, so that they are true priests of the New Testament. Partakers of the function of Christ the sole Mediator, (1 Tim 2:5) on their level of ministry, they announce the divine word to all. They exercise their sacred function especially in the Eucharistic worship or the celebration of the Mass by which acting in the person of Christ and proclaiming His Mystery they unite the prayers of the faithful with the sacrifice of their Head and renew and apply in the sacrifice of the Mass until the coming of the Lord (cf. 1 Cor. 11:26) the only sacrifice of the New Testament namely that of Christ offering Himself once for all a spotless Victim to the Father. (Cf. Heb. 9:11–28.) For the sick and the sinners among the faithful, they exercise the ministry of alleviation and reconciliation and they present the needs and the prayers of the faithful to God the Father. (Heb. 5:1–4) Exercising within the limits of their authority the function of Christ as Shepherd and Head, they gather together God's family as a brotherhood all of one mind, and lead them in the Spirit, through Christ, to God the Father. In the midst of the flock they adore Him in spirit and in truth. (Jn. 4:24) Finally, they labor in word and doctrine, (cf. 1 Tim. 5:17) believing what they have read and meditated upon in the law of God, teaching what they have believed, and putting in practice in their own lives what they have taught.[1] . . .

29. At a lower level of the hierarchy are deacons, upon whom hands are imposed "not unto the priesthood, but unto a ministry of service."[2] For strengthened by sacramental grace, in communion with the bishop and his group of priests they serve in the

sacerdotal Related to priests or priesthood.

diaconate of the liturgy, of the word, and of charity to the people of God. It is the duty of the deacon, according as it shall have been assigned to him by competent authority, to administer baptism solemnly, to be custodian and dispenser of the Eucharist, to assist at and bless marriages in the name of the Church, to bring **Viaticum** to the dying, to read the Sacred Scripture to the faithful, to instruct and exhort the people, to preside over the worship and prayer of the faithful, to administer sacramentals, to officiate at funeral and burial services. Dedicated to duties of charity and of administration, let deacons be mindful of the admonition of Blessed Polycarp: "Be merciful, diligent, walking according to the truth of the Lord, who became the servant of all."[3]

Endnotes

1. Ordo consecrationis sacerdotalis, in impositione vestimentorum. [Rite of Ordination of a Priest, at the clothing with vestments]
2. Constitutiones Ecclesiac aegyptiacae, III, 2: ed. Funk, Didascalia, II, p. 103. Statuta Eccl. Ant. 371: Mansi 3, 954.
3. S. Polycarpus, Ad Phil. 5, 2: ed. Funk, I, p. 300: Christus dicitur . omnium diaconus factus . Cfr. Didache, 15, 1: ib., p. 32. S.Ignatius M. Trall. 2, 3: ib., p. 242. Constitutiones Apostolorum, 8, 28, 4: ed. Funk, Didascalia, I, p. 530.

Excerpt from *On the Priesthood*
By Saint John Chrysostom

For the priestly office is indeed discharged on earth, but it ranks amongst heavenly ordinances; and very naturally so: for neither man, nor angel, nor archangel, nor any other created power, but the **Paraclete** Himself, instituted this vocation, and persuaded men while still abiding in the flesh to represent the ministry of angels. Wherefore the consecrated priest ought to be as pure as if he were standing in the heavens themselves in the midst of those powers. . . . Oh! what a marvel! what love of God to man! He who sitteth on high with the Father is at that hour held in the hands

Viaticum The Eucharist given to someone in immediate danger of death. Latin term means "with you on the way."

Paraclete In John's Gospel, the Holy Spirit is called the Paraclete, a Greek term for "advocate" or "counselor."

of all, and gives Himself to those who are willing to embrace and grasp Him. And this all do through the eyes of faith! Do these things seem to you fit to be despised, or such as to make it possible for any one to be uplifted against them?

Elijah and the Vast Multitude

The story of Elijah referred to here can be found in 1 Kings 18:21–40.

Would you also learn from another miracle the exceeding sanctity of this office? Picture Elijah and the vast multitude standing around him, and the sacrifice laid upon the altar of stones, and all the rest of the people hushed into a deep silence while the prophet alone offers up prayer: then the sudden rush of fire from Heaven upon the sacrifice:—these are marvellous things, charged with terror. Now then pass from this scene to the rites which are celebrated in the present day. . . . There stands the priest, not bringing down fire from Heaven, but the Holy Spirit: and he makes prolonged supplication, not that some flame sent down from on high may consume the offerings, but that grace descending on the sacrifice may thereby enlighten the souls of all. . . .

For if any one will consider how great a thing it is for one, being a man, and compassed with flesh and blood, to be enabled to draw nigh to that blessed and pure nature, he will then clearly see what great honor the grace of the Spirit has vouchsafed to priests; since by their agency these rites are celebrated. . . . For they who inhabit the earth and make their abode there are entrusted with

> 66 *There stands the priest, not bringing down fire from Heaven, but the Holy Spirit: and he makes prolonged supplication, not that some flame sent down from on high may consume the offerings, but that grace descending on the sacrifice may thereby enlighten the souls of all.* 99

the administration of things which are in Heaven, and have received an authority which God has not given to angels or archangels. For it has not been said to them, "Whatsoever ye shall bind on earth shall be bound in Heaven, and whatsoever ye shall loose on earth shall be loosed in Heaven." (Matt. 18:18) . . . For indeed what is it but all manner of heavenly authority which He has given them when He says, "Whose sins ye remit they are remitted, and whose sins ye retain they are retained?" (John 20:23) What authority could be greater than this? . . . For if no one can enter into the kingdom of Heaven except he be regenerate through water and the Spirit, and he who does not eat the flesh of the Lord and drink His blood is excluded from eternal life, and if all these things are accomplished only by means of those holy hands, I mean the hands of the priest, how will any one, without these, be able to escape the fire of hell, or to win those crowns which are reserved for the victorious?

These verily are they who are entrusted with the pangs of spiritual travail and the birth which comes through baptism: by their means we put on Christ, and are buried with the Son of God. . . . Wherefore they might not only be more justly feared by us than rulers and kings, but also be more honored than parents; since these begat us of blood and the will of the flesh, but the others are the authors of our birth from God, even that blessed regeneration which is the true freedom and the sonship according to grace. . . . Wherefore they who despise these priests would be far more accursed than Dathan and his company, and deserve more severe punishment. For the latter, although they laid claim to the dignity which did not belong to them, nevertheless had an excellent opinion concerning it, and this they evinced by the great eagerness with which they pursued it; but these men, when the office has been better regulated, and has received so great a development, have displayed an audacity which exceeds that of the others, although manifested in a contrary way. For there is not an equal amount of contempt involved in aiming at an honor which does not pertain to one, and in despising such great advantages, but the latter exceeds the former as much as scorn differs from admiration. What soul then is so sordid as to despise such great advantages? None whatever, I should say, unless it were one subject to some demoniacal impulse. For I return once more to the point from which I started: not in the way of chastising only, but also in the

> **Dathan and His Company**
>
> A group of Israelites, led by a man named Dathan, claimed that Moses was doing his own will and not the will of God (see Numbers 16:1–50).

way of benefiting, God has bestowed a power on priests greater than that of our natural parents. The two indeed differ as much as the present and the future life. For our natural parents generate us unto this life only, but the others unto that which is to come. And the former would not be able to avert death from their offspring, or to repel the assaults of disease; but these others have often saved a sick soul, or one which was on the point of perishing, procuring for some a milder chastisement, and preventing others from falling altogether, not only by instruction and admonition, but also by the assistance wrought through prayers. For not only at the time of regeneration, but afterwards also, they have authority to forgive sins. "Is any sick among you?" it is said, "let him call for the elders of the Church and let them pray over him, anointing him with oil in the name of the Lord. And the prayer of faith shall save the sick, and the Lord will raise him up: and if he have committed sins they shall be forgiven him." (James 5:14–15) Again: our natural parents, should their children come into conflict with any men of high rank and great power in the world, are unable to profit them: but priests have reconciled, not rulers and kings, but God Himself when His wrath has often been provoked against them.

Well! after this will any one venture to condemn me for arrogance? For my part, after what has been said, I imagine such religious fear will possess the souls of the hearers that they will no longer condemn those who avoid the office for arrogance and temerity, but rather those who voluntarily come forward and are eager to obtain this dignity for themselves. For if they who have been entrusted with the command of cities, should they chance to be wanting in discretion and vigilance, have sometimes destroyed the cities and ruined themselves in addition, how much power think you both in himself and from above must he need, to avoid sinning, whose business it is to beautify the Bride of Christ?

Excerpt from "From Communist Militant to Underground Priest: Father Bao's China Odyssey"

By Bao Yuanjin

My name is Bao Yuanjin and I'm a priest in China's north. I entered the priesthood several years ago. I was baptized only 11 years ago. Before that, I was an atheist, and indeed an activist in China's Communist Party. . . .

My life in the Communist cell was neither good nor bad. We students were good with everyone, studious and good at organizing all sorts of activities.

But I was struck by the fact that, in the Party, all these things, however good, were done not for the good of others, but for oneself, for the sake of career advancements. And then there were lies: These were the main feature among us: Everyone lied and everyone knew about the lies, but we carried on all the same. . . .

After some time, I became ill. I often had nightmares that even woke me from my sleep. One night, I dreamt that I found a package; I opened it and found a book in it. It was a Bible, all shining and bright. I woke up and recalled that my grandmother was the only person to have told me about the Bible. I remembered her saying that Jesus is all-powerful. . . .

[A] friend—who was Catholic, I later discovered—gave me 10 cassettes with recordings of the sermons of a Chinese priest. After having listened to the cassettes, a battle began to rage in my heart: I thought that perhaps God really exists; perhaps the Catholic religion is really the true one. . . .

I went to look for a Catholic Church and there I attended Mass, but always secretly. Bit by bit, I came to understand more about the Catholic faith and, in the end, decided to ask to be baptized. . . .

After becoming Catholic, I continued to attend Mass every Sunday, but with an underground community, not recognized by the government.

Once a nun said to me: Why don't you follow Jesus fully and become a priest? I said "no" right away. There are no believers in my family and becoming a priest would have been difficult.

As a firstborn child, I was obliged, by Chinese tradition, to support my parents in their old age. By entering a seminary, my first enemies would have been my parents.

Six months later, I was praying in my room when I heard a voice calling me: "Follow me." There was no one in the room. In my heart, I understood that it was Jesus calling me, but I was too frightened: Becoming a priest—of the underground Church—meant abandoning everything, leaving my family, my work, putting myself at risk, embracing the Cross, suffering, imprisonment.

I said no. But with my refusal, I no longer had peace as I became restless and lost all joy. I didn't want to follow Jesus since I had a good job, a quiet life. But I couldn't resist the Lord's call.

Thus, I prayed to find another job, in a city farther away. That way, I could leave my job less conspicuously and could enter the seminary. I worked in this other city for almost two years, to earn as much as possible, saving everything so that I could leave money for my parents and in the end I followed Jesus' call.

I knew that I was weak and so I prayed: "Jesus, if you want, you can make me faithful through and through, your disciple forever. This will be a very great miracle."

I spent five years in the seminary of the underground Church. Life was very difficult and very risky.

Wake-up time was 5 a.m. After a half-hour of meditation, we celebrated Mass and then lauds. After breakfast, we would clean up and then our studies would begin. We would go to bed at 10 p.m.

Life in an underground seminary is a bit hard: We lived in a country house made available to us by a member of the faithful.

But when we got news that the police had discovered us, we were forced to flee and settle in another place. In five years, we changed location three times.

We seminarians had to take care of the cleaning, but also the cooking, preparing meals for everyone. From the material standpoint, life was truly difficult: little food, few vegetables, hardly ever meat; crowded rooms with no extra space.

But, in my heart, I felt peace and even an entirely new joy, different from what I previously felt. There was a strong friendship and sense of brotherhood among the seminarians.

Difficulties were quickly overcome since everyone was ready to love each other.

After five years of study, the day came for my priestly ordination. There was a lot of tension at that time in my diocese and we risked being jailed by police. Thus, we celebrated the ordination Mass at 4 o'clock in the morning. At that time everyone in China is asleep, even the policemen.

Even if our life as Catholics is difficult, our faith truly strengthens us day after day. And this also thanks to the example of priests in prison.

One small example: In my hometown, in 1983, when China began its great economic reforms, there were only three Catholic families. Now, after almost 20 years, there are more than 4,000. It is really true that the blood of martyrs becomes the seed of new Christians.

For me too, my strength is Jesus himself. He said, "It was not you who chose me, but I who chose you" (John 15:16). Along this path, I find the Cross, but also joy and peace. With his help, I will always follow him, overcoming whatever difficulty that may arise.

For Reflection

1. All these readings present the priesthood as a noble and high calling. What personal characteristics do you think a person should have to become a priest?

2. Looking at the reading from John Chrysostom, how would you describe the greatness or the dignity of the priesthood?

3. The story of the Chinese priest Bao Yuanjin offers a glimpse of Church life under persecution. What do you think would motivate a person to become a priest under such circumstances?

17 The Sacrament of Matrimony

Introduction

The Gospel message is one of contradiction. Jesus says in Matthew 16:25, "For whoever wishes to save his life will lose it, but whoever loses his life for my sake will find it." Losing life, finding life. This great paradox is evident in the **Sacrament of Matrimony**. The starting point in the Church's theology of marriage is the love that Christ has for the Church. Jesus gave himself over to the most brutal suffering on behalf of the Church. It was the complete and total gift of himself.

Many people seem to enter marriage asking, "What can I get out of this relationship?" Perhaps that question focuses only on short-term satisfaction and not on the enduring, eternal nature of marriage. However, the Church asks married persons not to focus on themselves. The operative question is not, "What can I get from this person?" but rather, "Am I called to give my life for this particular person? Is this the person God asks me to give the gift of myself to?"

Marriage is a beautiful icon of the love Christ has for the Church. This Sacrament takes the human love between a woman and man and elevates it to a means of salvation. The man, the woman, and any children with which they are blessed have,

> **Sacrament of Matrimony** A lifelong covenant, modeled on that between Christ and the Church, in which a baptized man and a baptized woman make an exclusive and permanent commitment to faithfully love each other and to care for their children.

as their primary calling, to assist in one another's salvation. This concern is the foundation of a healthy marriage, a healthy family, and a healthy society.

This case is made in the readings from this chapter. The first reading, from *Pastoral Constitution on the Church in the Modern World* (*Gaudium et Spes,* 1965), from the Second Vatican Council, instructs the Church on how we should live in modern times. The council recognized that to instruct Christians on how to live, it needed to take a serious look at marriage and family. In the chapter's second reading, Pope John Paul II is concerned about the state of marriage and the family. He offers reflections on Matrimony in his apostolic exhortation *On the Role of the Christian Family in the Modern World (Familiaris Consortio)*, which flows from his landmark work *Theology of the Body.* Finally, the last reading tells the ordinary, yet profound, story of a married couple that demonstrates the beauty of lifelong selflessness.

Excerpt from *Pastoral Constitution on the Church in the Modern World (Gaudium et Spes)*

By the Second Vatican Council

Part II, Chapter I: Fostering the Nobility of Marriage and the Family

47. The well-being of the individual person and of human and Christian society is intimately linked with the healthy condition of that community produced by marriage and family. Hence Christians and all men who hold this community in high esteem sincerely rejoice in the various ways by which men today find help in fostering this community of love and perfecting its life, and by which parents are assisted in their lofty calling. Those who rejoice in such aids look for additional benefits from them and labor to bring them about.

Yet the excellence of this institution is not everywhere reflected with equal brilliance, since polygamy, the plague of divorce, so-called free love and other disfigurements have an obscuring effect. In addition, married love is too often profaned by excessive self-love, the worship of pleasure and illicit practices against human generation. Moreover, serious disturbances are caused in families by modern economic conditions, by influences at once social and psychological, and by the demands of civil society. Finally, in certain parts of the world problems resulting from population growth are generating concern.

All these situations have produced anxiety of consciences. Yet, the power and strength of the institution of marriage and family can also be seen in the fact that time and again, despite the difficulties produced, the profound changes in modern society reveal the true character of this institution in one way or another.

Therefore, by presenting certain key points of Church doctrine in a clearer light, this sacred synod wishes to offer guidance and support to those Christians and other men who are trying to preserve the holiness and to foster the natural dignity of the married state and its superlative value.

48. The intimate partnership of married life and love has been established by the Creator and qualified by His laws, and is rooted in the **conjugal** covenant of irrevocable personal consent. Hence by that human act whereby spouses mutually bestow and accept each other a relationship arises which by divine will and in the eyes of society too is a lasting one. For the good of the spouses and their off-springs as well as of society, the existence of the sacred bond no longer depends on human decisions alone. For, God Himself is the author of matrimony, endowed as it is with various benefits and purposes. All of these have a very decisive bearing on the continuation of the human race, on the personal development and eternal destiny of the individual members of a family, and on the dignity, stability, peace and prosperity of the family itself and of human society as a whole. By their very

conjugal Relating to marriage.

conjugal love The love reserved for wife and husband that is expressed in sexual union.

nature, the institution of matrimony itself and **conjugal love** are ordained for the procreation and education of children, and find in them their ultimate crown. Thus a man and a woman, who by their compact of conjugal love "are no longer two, but one flesh" (Matt. 19:ff), render mutual help and service to each other through an intimate union of their persons and of their actions. Through this union they experience the meaning of their oneness and attain to it with growing perfection day by day. As a mutual gift of two persons, this intimate union and the good of the children impose total fidelity on the spouses and argue for an unbreakable oneness between them.

Christ the Lord abundantly blessed this many-faceted love, welling up as it does from the fountain of divine love and structured as it is on the model of His union with His Church. For as God of old made Himself present (Cf. Hosea 2; Jer. 3:6–13; Ezech.16 and 23; Is. 54) to His people through a covenant of love and fidelity, so now the Savior of men and the Spouse (Cf. Matt. 9:15; Mark 2:19–20; Luke 5:34–35; John 3:29; Cf. also 2 Cor. 11:2; Eph. 5:27; Rev. 19:7–8; 21:2 and 9) of the Church comes into the lives of married Christians through the sacrament of matrimony. He abides with them thereafter so that just as He loved the Church and handed Himself over on her behalf, (Cf. Eph. 5:25) the spouses may love each other with perpetual fidelity through mutual self-bestowal.

Authentic married love is caught up into divine love and is governed and enriched by Christ's redeeming power and the saving activity of the Church, so that this love may lead the spouses to God with powerful effect and may aid and strengthen them in sublime office of being a father or a mother. For this reason Christian spouses have a special sacrament by which they are fortified and receive a kind of consecration in the duties and dignity of their state. By virtue of this sacrament, as spouses fulfil their conjugal and family obligation, they are penetrated with the spirit of Christ, which suffuses their whole lives with faith, hope and charity. Thus they increasingly advance the perfection of their own personalities, as well as their mutual sanctification, and hence contribute jointly to the glory of God.

As a result, with their parents leading the way by example and family prayer, children and indeed everyone gathered around the family hearth will find a readier path to human maturity, salvation and holiness. Graced with the dignity and office of fatherhood and motherhood, parents will energetically acquit themselves of a duty which devolves primarily on them, namely education and especially religious education.

As living members of the family, children contribute in their own way to making their parents holy. For they will respond to the kindness of their parents with sentiments of gratitude, with love and trust. They will stand by them as children should when hardships overtake their parents and old age brings its loneliness. Widowhood, accepted bravely as a continuation of the marriage vocation, (Cf. 1 Tim. 5:3) should be esteemed by all. Families too will share their spiritual riches generously with other families. Thus the Christian family, which springs from marriage as a reflection of the loving covenant uniting Christ with the Church, (Cf. Eph. 5:32) and as a participation in that covenant, will manifest to all men Christ's living presence in the world, and the genuine nature of the Church. This the family will do by the mutual love of the spouses, by their generous fruitfulness, their solidarity and faithfulness, and by the loving way in which all members of the family assist one another.

> " *Thus the Christian family, which springs from marriage as a reflection of the loving covenant uniting Christ with the Church, and as a participation in that covenant, will manifest to all men Christ's living presence in the world, and the genuine nature of the Church.* "

Excerpt from the Apostolic Exhortation *On the Role of the Christian Family in the Modern World (Familiaris Consortio)*

By Pope John Paul II

Part Two

The Plan of God for Marriage and the Family

Man, the Image of the God Who Is Love

11. God created man in His own image and likeness (Cf. Gn. 1:26–27): calling him to existence through love, He called him at the same time for love.

God is love (1 Jn. 4:8) and in Himself He lives a mystery of personal loving communion. Creating the human race in His own image and continually keeping it in being, God inscribed in the humanity of man and woman the vocation, and thus the capacity and responsibility, of love and communion. Love is therefore the fundamental and innate vocation of every human being.

As an incarnate spirit, that is a soul which expresses itself in a body and a body informed by an immortal spirit, man is called to love in his unified totality. Love includes the human body, and the body is made a sharer in spiritual love.

Christian revelation recognizes two specific ways of realizing the vocation of the human person in its entirety, to love: marriage and virginity or celibacy. Either one is, in its own proper form, an actuation of the most profound truth of man, of his being "created in the image of God."

Consequently, sexuality, by means of which man and woman give themselves to one another through the acts which are proper and exclusive to spouses, is by no means something purely biological, but concerns the innermost being of the human person as such. It is realized in a truly human way only if it is an integral part of the love by which a man and a woman commit themselves totally to one another until death. The total physical self-giving would be a lie if it were not the sign and fruit of a total personal self-giving, in which the whole person, including the temporal dimension, is present: if the person were to withhold something or reserve the possibility of deciding otherwise in the future, by this very fact he or she would not be giving totally.

This totality which is required by conjugal love also corresponds to the demands of responsible fertility. This fertility is directed to the generation of a human being, and so by its nature it surpasses the purely biological order and involves a whole series of personal values. For the harmonious growth of these values a persevering and unified contribution by both parents is necessary.

The only "place" in which this self-giving in its whole truth is made possible is marriage, the covenant of conjugal love freely and consciously chosen, whereby man and woman accept the intimate community of life and love willed by God Himself which only in this light manifests its true meaning. The institution of marriage is not an undue interference by society or authority, nor the extrinsic imposition of a form. Rather it is an interior requirement of the covenant of conjugal love which is publicly affirmed as unique and exclusive, in order to live in complete fidelity to the plan of God, the Creator. A person's freedom, far from being restricted by this fidelity, is secured against every form of subjectivism or relativism and is made a sharer in creative Wisdom. . . .

> *God inscribed in the humanity of man and woman the vocation, and thus the capacity and responsibility, of love and communion. Love is therefore the fundamental and innate vocation of every human being.*

13. The communion between God and His people finds its definitive fulfillment in Jesus Christ, the Bridegroom who loves and gives Himself as the Savior of humanity, uniting it to Himself as His body.

He reveals the original truth of marriage, the truth of the "beginning," (Cf. Gn.2:24; Mt. 19:5) and, freeing man from his hardness of heart, He makes man capable of realizing this truth in its entirety.

This revelation reaches its definitive fullness in the gift of love which the Word of God makes to humanity in assuming a human nature, and in the sacrifice which Jesus Christ makes of Himself on the Cross for His bride, the Church. In this sacrifice there is entirely revealed that plan which God has imprinted on the humanity of man and woman since their creation; (Cf. Eph. 5:32–33) the marriage of baptized persons thus becomes a real symbol of that new and eternal covenant sanctioned in the blood of Christ. The Spirit which the Lord pours forth gives a new heart, and renders man and woman capable of loving one another as Christ has loved us. Conjugal love reaches that fullness to which it is interiorly ordained, conjugal charity, which is the proper and specific way in which the spouses participate in and are called to live the very charity of Christ who gave Himself on the Cross.

In a deservedly famous page, **Tertullian** has well expressed the greatness of this conjugal life in Christ and its beauty: "How can I ever express the happiness of the marriage that is joined together by the Church[,] strengthened by an offering, sealed by a blessing, announced by angels and ratified by the Father? . . . How wonderful the bond between two believers with a single hope, a single desire, a single observance, a single service! They are both brethren and both fellow-servants; there is no separation between them in spirit or flesh; in fact they are truly two in one flesh and where the flesh is one, one in the spirit."[1]

Receiving and meditating faithfully on the word of God, the Church has solemnly taught and continues to teach that the marriage of the baptized is one of the seven sacraments of the New Covenant. Indeed, by means of baptism, man and woman are definitively placed within the new and eternal covenant, in the spousal covenant of Christ with the Church. And it is because of this indestructible insertion that the intimate community of conjugal life and love, founded by the Creator, is elevated and assumed into the spousal charity of Christ, sustained and enriched by His redeeming power.

Endnote

1. Tertullian, *Ad Uxorem*, II, VIII, 6–8: CCL, I, 393.

Excerpt from "CB and Helen," from *Pastoral Foundations of the Sacraments: A Catholic Perspective*

By Gregory L. Klein and Robert A. Wolfe

CB had been called CB for so long that he had just about forgotten about why he was called that. He remembered with a smile how it had come about. He and Helen met when they were in high school. They fell in love, as teenagers will, with incredible intensity. They just enjoyed each other's company. It wasn't long before they began to talk about how they would want to be together all the days of their lives. Helen was very affectionate. CB was stalky and practical. When CB would let the matter-of-facts of life dampen his spirit, Helen would always hug him and call him her "cuddly bear." CB, being really embarrassed when Helen called him that in public, asked her to stop calling him "cuddly bear," and thus he was named CB, and no one was supposed to know that under his practical, no-nonsense demeanor was truly a cuddly bear.

They were inseparable. Many times their parents complained that they were too intense and perhaps they needed to meet other people. Perhaps they were too young to be getting so deeply involved. Neither would listen to the advice given them. They began very early on to talk about marriage and children and growing up together. CB had always thought that the only practical thing to do was to get married. However, it was Helen who convinced him that they should wait until they were more mature. This waiting was the most difficult thing CB had ever done.

They decided that they would marry when they both turned twenty-one. The only problem with that was it gave CB a lot of time to worry about the consequences of being married. Would he be able to provide for Helen? If they had children, would he be a good father? What if he got attracted to someone else? Could he be faithful forever? The questions and the fears began to increase as the months and years unfolded toward their wedding day. When he would get particularly worked up, Helen would take him by the hand and remind him gently, "You are my CB and I can't live without you." CB would sigh and smile and realize that he couldn't live without Helen either.

They married. They had five children. They became successful. They struggled, worried, fought, and from time to time, had a really good time together. The years of their marriage passed like the pages of a good book. They were good people. He was practical. She was sensitive. They were preparing to celebrate their golden anniversary.

Months before the day, CB became really fascinated with the idea of marking fifty years together. After dinner he would sit before the TV and muse about the many events that made the story of their marriage. From time to time he would get nostalgic and sometimes melancholy as he would remember the difficult times. Helen would just reach out to him and touch his arm and say, "Remember, you are my CB." That was always enough.

CB wanted a big celebration. He wanted all his friends and all of his children and grandchildren to come together for a big party. He was successful. He could afford it. Helen refused. She said, "I'm an old lady now. I don't want everyone looking at me." She suggested that they just go to Mass together on the anniversary day and have the priest give them a blessing. That would be enough. She would make him a wonderful breakfast afterward.

CB loved her more after fifty years than he did when they first made marriage vows. He wanted to do something special. He wanted to be impractical and romantic. Helen refused the party. She also refused his offer to buy her a new ring. "I have held on to this ring for fifty years. I look at it every day and remember the promises I made to you. I don't want to be looking at any other ring."

CB wanted desperately to do something special for their anniversary day. He finally settled on doing something they had done their whole married life. For birthdays and holidays, on sick days and celebration days, he would buy her a card from the card shop. He always liked the pictures on the outside and never paid much attention to the greeting on the inside. They were always good. He figured he had bought a thousand cards over the years. He would choose a card he liked and often without reading the sentiments inside would sign it, "Your CB."

CB knew that Helen would accept a card from him for the anniversary. He would pick the perfect card and sign it and give it to her at the door of the church where they were married fifty years earlier.

He spent a long time at the card store. He was surprised at how many choices there were. He looked for the most beautiful card that would express his love. After a long time he chose a card that pictured a mature couple holding hands and walking down a country road. The outside of the card said, "Beloved, our journey together has been wonderful!" CB thought it was perfect.

As he prepared for bed on the night of his anniversary, CB remembered that he needed to sign the card. He left Helen in the bedroom and went to the kitchen. He took a glass of milk and looked at his card for a long time. He remembered a lot and cried a little. He finally opened the card to sign it and was horrified. The card was blank. Nothing, no greeting, no romantic words were written there. He panicked. What could he do at the last moment? Finally, he took up a pen and wrote—

> My dearest Helen,
> Take me by the arm today because with you I have never been afraid. I thank God for you every day of my life. I cannot imagine life without you. I promise you that I will take your arm tomorrow and God will bless me as he has done for many years.
> With all my love,
> Your CB

For Reflection

1. *Pastoral Constitution on the Church in the Modern World* says children assist their parents' growth in holiness. How do you think you can help your parents or guardians grow in holiness?

2. Pope John Paul II says, "Love is therefore the fundamental and innate vocation of every human being" (11). Do you agree with this statement? Explain.

3. Later in this same paragraph, Pope John Paul II writes, "The total physical self-giving would be a lie if it were not the sign and fruit of a total personal self-giving. . . ." What do think this means for today's teens?

4. The readings show that marriage is a symbol of Christ's love for the Church. The love of Christ led to his total self-gift on the cross. Do you think married people realize they are to be total gifts to each other? How would you interpret this idea for a couple preparing for Matrimony?

For Further Reading

The Church documents, writings from the Doctors of the Church, and the stories excerpted in this book represent only a small part of the Catholic writings on the Sacraments. A sample of additional writings follows, arranged to correspond to each chapter. The documents of the Second Vatican Council are available online at the Vatican Web site (*www.vatican.va*). The Church's documents that defined the official teaching on the Sacraments were originally written in Latin. In these cases every effort has been made to find accessible English translations. In addition to the documents of the Church, writings from the Doctors of the Church have been recommended, as have writings from contemporary theologians. For works of prose, *Great Catholic Writings: Thought, Literature, Spirituality, Social Action,* by Robert Feduccia Jr. and others (Winona, MN: Saint Mary's Press, 2006), contains good and lengthier selections that bring the Sacraments to life.

For a deeper theological read from a contemporary Catholic perspective, *Systematic Theology: Roman Catholic Perspectives,* volumes I and II, edited by Francis Schüssler Fiorenza and John P. Galvin (Minneapolis: Fortress, 1991) is highly recommended. The second volume deals specifically with the Sacraments. The articles are written at an adult level, but they are geared to college readers rather than to scholars. Many of the following works have been recommended in those volumes.

Part 1: The Sacramental Nature of the Church

Chapters 1–7:

Cross, Frank L., ed. *St. Cyril of Jerusalem's Lectures on the Christian Sacraments: The Procatechesis and the Five Mystagogical Catecheses.* Crestwood, NY: St. Vladimir Press, 1986.

Dulles, Avery. *Models of the Church.* New York: Random House (Image Book), 2002.

Ganoczy, Alexandra. *An Introduction to Catholic Sacramental Theology.* New York: Paulist Press, 1984.

Martinez, German. *Signs of Freedom: Theology of the Christian Sacraments.* Mahwah, NJ: Paulist Press, 2003.

Martos, Joseph. *Doors to the Sacred: A Historical Introduction to the Sacraments in the Catholic Church.* Ligouri, MO: Ligouri / Triumph, 2001.

Rahner, Karl. *The Church and the Sacraments.* New York: Herder, 1963.

Ratzinger, Joseph. *The Spirit of the Liturgy.* San Francisco: Ignatius Press, 2000.

Schillebeeckx, Edward. *Christ the Sacrament of the Encounter with God.* New York: Sheed and Ward, 1962.

Part 2: The Sacraments of Christian Initiation

Chapter 8: Christian Initiation: The Beginning of Christian Life

Dejarier, Michel, and Kevin Hart. *The Rites of Christian Initiation: Historical and Pastoral Reflections.* New York: Sadlier, 1979.

National Council of Catholic Bishops. *Rite of Christian Initiation of Adults.* Chicago: Liturgy Training Publications, 1988.

Osborne, Kenan. *The Christian Sacraments of Initiation.* Mahwah, NJ: Paulist Press, 1987.

Yarnold, Edward. *The Awe-inspiring Rites of Initiation: The Origins of R.C.I.A.* Slough, UK: St. Paul Publications, 1971.

Chapter 9: The Sacrament of Baptism

Fischer, J. D. C. *Christian Initiation: Baptism in the Medieval West.* London: SPCK, 1970.

Kavanaugh, Aidan. *The Shape of Baptism.* New York: Pueblo, 1978.

Stasiak, Kurt. *Return to Grace: A Theology of Infant Baptism.* Collegeville, MN: Liturgical Press, 1996.

Whitaker, E. C., ed. *Documents of the Baptismal Liturgy.* London: SPCK, 1981.

Chapter 10: The Sacrament of Confirmation

Austin, Gerard. *The Rite of Confirmation: Anointing with the Spirit.* Collegeville, MN: Liturgical Press, 1985.

Chupungco, Anscar J. *Handbook for Liturgical Studies: Sacraments and Sacramentals,* vol. IV. Collegeville, MN: Liturgical Press, 2000.

Kavanaugh, Aidan. *Confirmation: Origins and Reform.* New York: Pueblo, 1988.

McDonnell, Kilian, and George T. Montague. *Christian Initiation and Baptism in the Holy Spirit: Evidence from the First Eight Centuries.* Collegeville, MN: Liturgical Press, 1990.

Chapter 11: The Sacrament of the Eucharist

Bouyer, Louis, translated by Charles Underhill Quinn. *Eucharist: The Theology and Spirituality of the Eucharistic Prayer.* Notre Dame, IN: Notre Dame Press, 1968.

Léon-Dufour, Xavier. *Sharing the Eucharistic Bread: The Witness of the New Testament.* New York: Paulist Press, 1987.

Ratzinger, Joseph. *The Spirit of the Liturgy.* San Francisco: Ignatius Press, 2000.

Rordorf, Willy, translated by Matthew O'Connell. *The Eucharist of the Early Christians.* New York: Pueblo, 1978.

Part 3: The Sacraments of Healing

Chapter 12: Healing of Soul and Body

Glennon, A. J. *The Theology of Healing.* Gerrigong, NSW, Australia: Order of St. Luke the Physician, 1978.

O'Meara, Thomas. *Theology of Ministry.* New York: Paulist Press, 1983.

Poschmann, Bernard, translated by Francis Courtney. *Penance and the Anointing of the Sick.* New York: Herder and Herder, 1964.

Ratzinger, Joseph. *Called to Communion: Understanding the Church Today.* San Francisco: Ignatius Press, 1996.

Chapter 13: The Sacrament of Penance and Reconciliation

Dallen, James. *The Reconciling Community: The Rite of Penance.* New York: Pueblo, 1986.

Favazza, Joseph. *The Order of Penitents: Historical Roots and Pastoral Future.* Collegeville, MN: Liturgical Press, 1988.

Gula, Richard. *To Walk Together: The Sacrament of Reconciliation.* New York: Paulist Press, 1984.

Chapter 14: The Sacrament of Anointing of the Sick

Duffy, Regis. *A Roman Catholic Theology of Pastoral Care.* Philadelphia: Fortress, 1983.

Gusmer, Charles. *And You Visited Me: Sacramental Ministry to the Sick and Dying.* New York: Pueblo, 1984.

Knauber, Adolf. *A Pastoral Theology of the Anointing the Sick.* Collegeville, MN: Liturgical Press, 1975.

Rahner, Karl. *On the Theology of Death.* New York: Herder and Herder, 1961.

Part 4: The Sacraments at the Service of Communion

Chapter 15: The Baptismal Call to Holiness and Service

Dulles, Avery. *Models of the Church.* New York: Random House (Image Book), 2002.

O'Meara, Thomas. *Theology of Ministry.* New York: Paulist Press, 1983.

Schillebeeckx, Edward. *The Church with a Human Face: A New and Expanded Theology of Ministry.* New York: Crossroads, 1985.

Chapter 16: The Sacrament of Holy Orders

Cooke, Bernard. *Ministry to Word and Sacrament: History and Theology.* Philadelphia: Fortress, 1976.

Fisher, Saint John, translated by Stanley L. Jacki. *The Defense of the Priesthood.* Port Huron, MI: Real View Books, 1996.

Galot, Jean. *Theology of the Priesthood.* San Francisco: Ignatius Press, 1984.

International Theological Commission. *From the Diakonia of Christ to the Diakonia of the Apostles.* London: Catholic Truth Society, 2003.

Chapter 17: The Sacrament of Matrimony

Garcia de Haro, Ramon, translated by William E. May. *Marriage and the Family in the Documents of the Magisterium: A Course in the Theology of Marriage.* San Francisco: Ignatius Press, 1993.

Kasper, Walter. *Theology of Christian Marriage.* New York: Crossroads, 1983.

Mackin, Theodore. *The Marital Sacrament.* Mahwah, NJ: Paulist Press, 1989.

West, Christopher. *Theology of the Body Explained: A Commentary on John Paul II's "Gospel of the Body."* Boston: Pauline Books and Media, 2003.

Acknowledgments

Scripture texts used in this work are taken from the *New American Bible, revised edition* © 2010, 1991, 1986, 1970 Confraternity of Christian Doctrine, Inc., Washington, D.C. All Rights Reserved. No part of this work may be reproduced or transmitted in any form or by any means, electronic or mechanical, including photocopying, recording, or by any information storage and retrieval system, without permission in writing from the copyright owner.

The excerpts marked *Catechism* and *CCC* are from the English translation of the *Catechism of the Catholic Church* for use in the United States of America, second edition. Copyright © 1994 by the United States Catholic Conference, Inc.—Libreria Editrice Vaticana (LEV). English translation of the *Catechism of the Catholic Church: Modifications from the Editio Typica* copyright © 1997 by the United States Catholic Conference, Inc.—LEV.

The excerpt on pages 12–15 is from *The Sentences: Book 4*, by Peter Lombard, at *www.franciscan-archive.org/lombardus/opera/ls4-01*.

The quotations on pages 16 and 138–139 and the excerpts on pages 17–22, 55–56, 68–69, 139–142, and 152–156 are from *Dogmatic Constitution on the Church (Lumen Gentium*, 1964), numbers 1, 42, and 1, 2, 3, 4, 5, 7, 11, 7, 17, 40, 41, 18, 20, 21, 28, and 29, respectively, at *www.vatican.va/archive/hist_councils/ii_vatican_council/documents/vat-ii_const_19641121_lumen-gentium_en.html*. Copyright © LEV. Used with permission of LEV.

The quotations on page 24 and in reflection question 3 on page 28, and the excerpt on pages 24–28 are from *Christ the Sacrament of the Encounter with God*, by Edward Schillebeeckx (Kansas City, MO: Sheed and Ward, 1963), pages 54, 47, and 47–49 and 52–54, respectively. Copyright © 1963 by Sheed and Ward. Used with permission of Sheed and Ward, an imprint of Rowman and Littlefield Publishers.

The excerpt on pages 30–33 and the quotation in reflection question 4 on page 34 are from *Models of the Church*, expanded edition, by Avery

Dulles (New York: Doubleday, 1987), pages 67–70 and 70. Copyright © 1974, 1987 by Avery Dulles. Used with permission of Doubleday, a division of Random House, Inc.

The excerpt on pages 36–40 and in reflection question 3 on page 40 are from *Dogmatic Constitution on the Sacred Liturgy* (*Sacrosanctum Concilium*, 1963), numbers 1, 2, 7, 10, 11, 12, 14, and 11, respectively, at *www.vatican.va/archive/hist_councils/ii_vatican_council/documents/vat-ii_const_19631204_sacrosanctum-concilium_en.html*. Copyright © LEV. Used with permission of LEV.

The quotation on page 41 and the excerpt on pages 42–45 are from *The Spirit of the Liturgy*, by Joseph Cardinal Ratzinger, translated by John Saward (San Francisco: Ignatius Press, 2000), pages 57 and 53–57. Copyright © 2000 Ignatius Press. Used with permission of Ignatius Press.

The excerpt on pages 48–51 is from *The Dialogue of the Seraphic Virgin Catherine of Siena: Dictated by Her, While in a State of Ecstasy, to Her Secretaries, and Completed in the Year of Our Lord 1370, Together with an Account of Her Death by an Eye-Witness*, translated from the original Italian, and preceded by an introduction on the life and times of the saint, by Algar Thorold, new and abridged edition (London: Kegan Paul, Trench, Trubner and Co., 1907).

The excerpt on pages 56–60 and the quotation in reflection question 2 on page 63 are from "Christian Initiation: Gate to Salvation," by Monika Hellwig, in *Chicago Studies*, volume 22, number 3, November 1983. Copyright © Civitas Dei Foundation. Used with permission of Civitas Dei Foundation.

The excerpt on pages 60–63 is from "A Rite of Passage," by Aidan Kavanagh, delivered as part of a lecture at the Theology Institute at Holy Cross Abbey in Cannon City, Colorado, August 1977. Used with permission of Saint Meinrad Archabbey.

The excerpt on pages 66–68 is from *Decrees of the Ecumenical Councils*, edited by Norman P. Tanner (London: Sheed and Ward; Washington, DC: Georgetown University Press, 1990), pages 541–543 and 576–577. English translation copyright © 1990 by Sheed and Ward Limited and the Trustees for Roman Catholic Purposes Registered. Used with kind permission of Continuum International Publishing Group.

The quotation on page 65 and the excerpt on pages 69–73 are from "Homily of His Holiness Benedict XVI, Feast of the Baptism of the Lord," at *www.vatican.va/holy_father/benedict_xvi/homilies/2007/documents/ hf_ben-xvi_hom_20070107_battesimo_en.html*. Copyright © 2007 LEV. Used with permission of LEV.

The excerpts on pages 73–75 and 171–173 are from *Pastoral Foundations of the Sacraments: A Catholic Perspective*, by Gregory L. Klein and Robert A. Wolfe (New York / Mahwah, NJ: Paulist Press, 1988), pages 54–55 and 129–131. Copyright © 1998 by Gregory L. Klein and Robert A. Wolfe. Used with permission of Paulist Press, Inc., www.paulistpress.com.

The excerpt on pages 78–81 is from the English translation of "Apostolic Constitution on the Sacrament of Confirmation," from *Rite of Confirmation (Second Edition)* © 1975, International Committee on English in the Liturgy Corporation (ICEL), in *Rites of the Catholic Church*, volume one, prepared by the ICEL, a Joint Commission of Catholic Bishops' Conferences (Collegeville, MN: Liturgical Press, 1990), pages 472–474 and 477. Copyright © 1990, The Order of St. Benedict, Collegeville, MN. Used with permission of the ICEL. All rights reserved.

The excerpt on pages 81–85 and the quotation in reflection question 2 on page 87 are from "Address of His Holiness Benedict XVI on the Occasion of the 23rd World Youth Day, 2008," at *www.vatican.va/holy_father/ benedict_xvi/speeches/2008/july/documents/hf_ben-xvi_spe_20080719_vigil_ en.html*. Copyright © 2008 LEV. Used with permission of LEV.

The excerpt on pages 85–86 is from "What Difference Does Confirmation Make?" by Joseph Martos, at *www.americancatholic.org/Newsletters/ YU/ay0385.asp*. Used with permission of St. Anthony Messenger Press.

The excerpts on pages 90–93 and 114–118 are from *Canons and Decrees of the Council of Trent*, English translation by H. J. Schroeder (Rockford, IL: Tan Books and Publishers, 1978), pages 73, 74, 75, 76, 77–78 and 88, 90, 91, 92, 93, 95, and 97, respectively.

The excerpt on pages 94–96 is from *De Fide Orthodoxa*, Book 4, Chapter 13, by St. John Damascene, at *mb-soft.com/believe/txud/damasc24.htm*.

The excerpt on pages 96–98 is from "Homily of Jean Vanier at Lambeth Vigil (Second Service)," at *www.lambethconference.org/1998/news/ lc088.cfm*. Used with permission of the Anglican Consultative Council.

The quotation on page 102 and the excerpt on pages 103–106 are from "Decree *Ad Gentes* on the Mission Activity of the Church," numbers 1, 3, 8, and 9, respectively, at *www.vatican.va/archive/hist_councils/ ii_vatican_council/documents/vat-ii_decree_19651207_ad-gentes_en.html*. Copyright © LEV. Used with permission of LEV.

The excerpt on pages 106–108 is from *Signs of Freedom: Theology of the Christian Sacraments*, by German Martinez (New York / Mahwah, NJ: Paulist Press, 2004), pages 223–224. Copyright © 2003 by German Martinez. Used with permission of Paulist Press, Inc., www.paulistpress.com.

The excerpt on pages 109–111 is from *The Wisdom of Accepted Tenderness: Going Deeper into the Abba Experience,* by Brennan Manning (Denville, NJ: Dimension Books, 1978), pages 60–63. Copyright © 1978 by Brennan Manning. Used with permission of the author.

The quotation on page 113 and the excerpt on pages 118–120 are from *Ante-Nicene Fathers: Translations of the Writings of the Fathers Down to AD 325*, volume five: *Hippolytus, Cyprian, Caius, Novatian, Appendix,* Alexander Roberts and James Donaldson, editors, revised and chronologically arranged by A. Cleveland Coxe (New York: Christian Literature Publishing Company, 1886).

The excerpt on pages 121–122 is from "The Evangelistic Power of Sacraments," by Shaun Gowney, at *www.ccr.org.uk/testimon/shaun.htm.* Used with permission of the author and *Good News Magazine.*

The excerpt on pages 125–128 is from *On the Sacrament of Anointing of the Sick (Sacram Unctione Infirmorum),* at *www.vatican.va/holy_father/ paul_vi/apost_constitutions/documents/hf_p-vi_apc_19721130_sacram-unctionem_en.html.* Copyright © LEV. Used with permission of LEV.

The excerpt on pages 128–130 is from *Systematic Theology: Roman Catholic Perspectives*, Volume II, Francis Schüssler Fiorenza and John P. Galvin, editors (Minneapolis: Fortress Press, 1991), pages 254–256. Copyright © 1991 Augsburg Fortress. Used with permission of Augsburg Fortress. All rights reserved.

The excerpt on pages 130–134 and the quotation in reflection question 3 on page 135 are from "Rest Assured: The Anointing of the Sick," by John Shea, in *US Catholic*, February 1, 1999. Copyright © 1999 by Claretian Publications. Used with permission of *US Catholic.*

The excerpt on pages 143–147 is from "Apostolic Letter, *Dilecti Amici*, of Pope John Paul II to the Youth of the World on the Occasion of International Youth Year," numbers 8, 9, and 10, respectively, at *www.vatican.va/holy_father/john_paul_ii/apost_letters/documents/hf_jp-ii_apl_31031985_dilecti-amici_en.html*. Copyright © 2007 LEV. Used with permission of LEV.

The excerpt on pages 147–149 is from "Vocation Story," by Gale Hammerschmidt, at *salinadiocese.org/vocations/seminarians/gales-vocation-story*. Used with permission of the author.

The excerpt on pages 149–150 is from *Marriage and Family: A Christian Theological Foundation,* by Natalie Kertes Weaver (Winona, MN: Anselm Academic, 2009), pages 146–147. Copyright © 2009 by Natalie Kertes Weaver. Used with permission of Anselm Academic.

The quotation on page 152 and the excerpt on pages 156–159 are from *A Select Library of Nicene and Post-Nicene Fathers of the Christian Church*, [first series], volume 9: *St. Chrysostom: On the Priesthood, Ascetic Treatises, Select Homilies and Letters, Homilies on the Statutes*, edited by Philip Schaff (New York: Christian Literature Publishing Company, 1886).

The excerpt on pages 160–162 is from "From Communist Militant to Underground Priest: Father Bao's China Odyssey," at *www.zenit.org/article-13403?l=english*.

The excerpt on pages 164–167 is from *Pastoral Constitution on the Church in the Modern World (Gaudium et Spes, 1965)*, numbers 47–48, at *www.vatican.va/archive/hist_councils/ii_vatican_council/documents/vat-ii_cons_19651207_gaudium-et-spes_en.html*. Copyright © LEV. Used with permission of LEV.

The excerpt on pages 168–170 and the quotations in reflection questions 2 and 3 on page 174 are from *On the Role of the Christian Family in the Modern World (Familiaris Consortio)*, numbers 11, 13, and 11, respectively, at *www.vatican.va/holy_father/john_paul_ii/apost_exhortations/documents/hf_jp-ii_exh_19811122_familiaris-consortio_en.html*. Copyright © LEV. Used with permission of LEV.

To view copyright terms and conditions for Internet materials cited here, log on to the home pages for the referenced Web sites.

During this book's preparation, all citations, facts, figures, names, addresses, telephone numbers, Internet URLs, and other pieces of information cited within were verified for accuracy. The authors and Saint Mary's Press staff have made every attempt to reference current and valid sources, but we cannot guarantee the content of any source, and we are not responsible for any changes that may have occurred since our verification. If you find an error in, or have a question or concern about, any of the information or sources listed within, please contact Saint Mary's Press.

Endnote Cited in a Quotation from the *Catechism of the Catholic Church,* Second Edition

1. Cf. Council of Vienne (1312): Denzinger-Schönmetzer, *Enchiridion Symbolorum, definitionum et declarationum de rebus fidei et morum* (1965) 902.